1981.

To John.

Fifty tries scored
Now for the fifty Runs.

Best Wishes

Connie & Alan

The Men in White

THE STORY OF ENGLISH RUGBY

Also available

THE MEN IN SCARLET
THE STORY OF WELSH RUGBY FOOTBALL
J. B. G. Thomas

THE MEN IN GREEN
THE STORY OF IRISH RUGBY
Sean Diffley

The Men in White

THE STORY OF ENGLISH RUGBY

Wallace Reyburn

PELHAM BOOKS

First published in Great Britain by
PELHAM BOOKS LTD
52 Bedford Square
London, WC1B 3EF
1975

ISBN 0 7207 0831 1

Set and printed in Great Britain by
Tonbridge Printers Ltd
Peach Hall Works, Tonbridge, Kent
in Baskerville eleven on twelve point
on paper supplied by P. F. Bingham Ltd
and bound by James Burn, Esher

Contents

Illustrations

1. White With a Red Rose

There is of course something special about England as far as rugby is concerned. After all, they invented the game. They formed the first Union. They played in the first International, although actually it was not their idea to start what in the Southern Hemisphere are called Tests, a term which is creeping into British rugby parlance because it gets around the confusion of 'an International' meaning at one and the same time a match and a person who plays in that match.

From the outset the men who have represented England in such matches (more than 1,000 by now) have always played in white, for no other reason than that the gentlemen who got the first England team together decided that that was the way it would be – all white with a simple red rose as emblem. It is a good looking strip. More than that, it is unique in international rugby in that it has never changed, is never even temporarily altered for a match due to colour clash or the desire of TV producers to prevent the owners of black-and-white sets from being in a state of complete confusion as to what is happening on their screens.

South Africa messed around with readily available local jerseys before getting their green with springbok emblem in 1906. New Zealand first played in blue, then on the formation of their Rugby Union in 1893 decided on black jersey with white shorts, only to alter that for the First All Blacks of 1905. The British Isles, having used all sorts of variations of red-white-and-blue strips for their early tours, sent the 1930 Lions to New Zealand in blue with white shorts. This annoyed the New Zealanders because it meant that for the

Tests their side had to avoid a colour clash and depart from the beloved all black, turning out in white with black shorts. So that it wouldn't happen again the Lions on their next tour adopted the red we know today. Australia, with almost identical strip as South Africa, solved the constant colour clash by switching to Old Gold jerseys and green shorts in 1961.

While all this was going on, England were always the Men in White, and still are. They have never needed to change for anybody. Wales so often have to switch from white to black shorts to keep the TV viewers happy. Ireland play in all white against South Africa for the same reason. Scotland, whose strip is the neatest, they look the most well groomed when they take the field, have to change to white against South Africa (for TV) and the same against the All Blacks to avoid their dark blue being confusing for the referee. Poor France always seem to get the shifty end of the stick. They have the most colourful gear of the lot but nowadays never seem to have the chance to wear it. Perhaps because they are the junior members of the International set, it always seems to be they who have to abandon their lively strip when colour clash or the demands of TV dictate. *Ce n'est pas juste.*

If England's immaculate white hasn't changed, plenty of other things about her rugby have.

We'll see how the game which in this country was essentially a pastime of the public school and varsity type is now embraced by young men of the sorts who formerly would have thought only in terms of soccer and would have looked with something akin to derision at the 'rugger' fraternity. Result: the game is booming. The total of 1,010 clubs affiliated to the Rugby Football Union immediately after the war had jumped to 2,165 in the 1970s. And this was not merely a reflection of a general upsurge of interest in sport. On the contrary, television addiction and the love affair the English are now carrying on with the motor car – the two factors which have most changed the English way of life in the post-war era – not only closed cinemas by the hundreds but also have been responsible for a falling away in support of team sports such as cricket, soccer and Rugby

League. Commercial sponsors had to step in to do a rescue act for cricket, with one-day tournaments. Dwindling soccer gates have many soccer clubs facing bankruptcy. Widespread disinterest in Rugby League has meant that they cannot even fill a medium-sized ground for their Internationals. And in the face of this, rugby goes from strength to strength.

We shall see that a contribution to the boom is the fact that English rugby – always considered a soft touch on both regional and national level by the once mighty Springboks and All Blacks – is now definitely not so. English sides have been doing some winning, thanks mainly to the radical change in attitude towards preparing for matches. The casual approach to the game, which was all right for playing consistent losing rugby against the dedicated invaders, has now been replaced by coaching, training and determined effort to be proficient in the basic skills. This, combined with some very sensible law changes by the International Board which make for much more open rugby, has made it a much better game to play and to watch – with more and more people wanting to do each.

2. *England Invents Rugby*

It is difficult to think of many international sports that did not come out of Britain. The Americans took England's rounders and turned it into baseball and evolved basketball from England's netball. The Canadians developed lacrosse from a pastime of their Indians. But in trying to think of other non-British sports that have any sort of impact around the world one becomes rather hard-pressed. Pelota? Korfball?

The really big ones all got their start here. Giving a nod to the Scots for golf, it is the English who have been far and away the world's most inventive when it comes to sport. Soccer, law tennis, cricket, hockey, modern boxing and athletics, badminton, bowls . . . all are English products and in the majority of cases these sports as we know them today were the outcome of the English sense of orderliness. Cricket is an exception. The English conjured that one up out of thin air, giving the world a game the like of which had never existed before. But things like tennis, boxing and athletics had existed in some form or other previously. The English merely stepped in and got them organised, drew up rules and regulations and laid down specifications as to sizes and types of playing area and equipment. If they hadn't, tennis today might still mean bashing a ball against the walls of a mock-up of the courtyard of a French chateau.

Rugby football, the notable absentee from my list of English creations above, was similarly not a pure invention out of nothing, as was cricket. Football of a type existed in Roman times and there is every reason to believe that it was the Romans who brought to England the idea of kicking a ball around for pleasure. By the Middle Ages, however, 'pleasure' was hardly the operative word since in the town games which consisted of hundreds of people chasing through the streets had become so violent that it came to be described as 'a bloody murthering practice'.

In the 18th century efforts to organise these street matches into games played between teams of limited numbers were not always successful, the onlookers having difficulty in resisting the temptation to join in. But by the start of the 19th century football was to take on more orderly shape and there is a point that should be made at this stage. Many people are under the impression that by this time soccer in something like the form we know it today had come into being and it was while playing in a soccer match that a boy at Rugby School made a name for himself by picking up the ball and running with it, thus sowing the seed for a new game which was to become known as rugby. In point of fact soccer and rugby were developing side by side, being differentiated then as the 'dribbling' and the 'handling' game.

Football had become popular at the public schools and which form of it was embraced at each particular school was dictated very much by the playing area available. In the cloisters at Charterhouse, for example, it was much safer to stick to dribbling on the flagged pavement. The wide open grass playground at Rugby lent itself to handling the ball and 'collaring' by opponents.

In 1823 when William Webb Ellis was said to have performed the exploit which is generally accepted as the starting point of rugby football the rules of the game at Rugby laid down that when a player made a fair catch opponents could not advance beyond that mark, while he withdrew either to punt or for the ball to be held on the ground for a place kick. On that historic day in 1823 Ellis, with what the plaque at the school commemorates as 'a fine disregard for the rules of football as played in his time', elected to run with the ball at his opponents instead of retiring with it.

Although at the time regarded as a rather caddish thing to do, it caught on with the boys as an exciting new variation to a game which by then had become rather bogged down in interminable mauls, relieved only occasionally by kicks at goal. At that stage of the sport's development the only way to score points was with goal kicks and it is interesting how the word 'try' came into rugby language with its present meaning.

When the attacking side achieved a *touchdown* (a word American football had persisted with, rather than adopting rugby's *try*) it carried no points, merely entitling the team to have a try at kicking a goal. When their side made a touchdown gleeful spectators naturally shouted 'A try!', which gradually took over as a neater little word to designate the touching of the ball down over the opponents' goal line, plus avoiding confusion with a defensive touchdown by a team in their own in-goal area.

It was a long time before it was recognised that scoring a try was an achievement in itself worthy of being awarded points. Goals (kicking the ball between the posts above the crossbar by any means except a punt) were always the deciding factor, until in 1875 it was ruled that matches could be decided on a majority of tries if the goals were equal or none had been kicked. But then at last the try got its just recognition in 1886 when an elementary points system was introduced. Modern scoring (except of course for the later variations as to drop-kick and try) came in 1905.

But let us return to the 1820s and the boys at Bigside, on the playing fields of Rugby. The idea of 'running in', as started by William Webb Ellis became more and more popular and eventually the rules of the game at the school were changed. Running towards your opponents' goal rather than having to kick after a catch on the full was legalised. Then it was permitted to do it 'on the bound' (from a bouncing ball) and at length it was permitted when you gained possession by any means. And thus gradually the game that had been predominantly mauls and kicks gave place to the running game as we know rugby today.

From the school the game spread, mainly through the efforts of old Rugbeians keen to carry on with it after they had left. Arthur Pell, a Cambridge undergraduate who was later to become an M.P., got it going at the university in 1839. The first rugby club to have been formed is said to have been at Guy's Hospital in 1843 but this is questioned by Dublin University where it is claimed that their's of 1854 was the first on the basis that the Guy's Hospital claim is not sufficiently documented. Be that as it may, the Scottish first was definitely Edinburgh Academicals, in 1858. The Public School and varsity atmosphere, in which rugby was to take root and thrive, did not loom large in the Welsh way of life, so that in Wales the formation of the first club did not come until much later, with the starting of the Neath club in 1871. By then the inauguration of English clubs similarly not directly associated with Public Schools and universities was well under way – Blackheath, formed in 1862, Richmond (1863), Bradford, Liverpool and Harlequins (1866) and Wasps (1867).

The spread of the game overseas does not come within this book's terms of reference, but as a matter of interest New Zealand got its first rugby club in 1870 and South Africa in 1875. It is puzzling why these two great rugby countries embraced the handling game rather than soccer, which would have been far more logical in view of the fact that among early British colonists soccer enthusiasts must surely have far outnumbered the rugger types. But by the same token why did Aussies in the rough-and-ready pioneer days latch on so wholeheartedly to cricket, which one would have thought would have been something far too genteel for those rugged customers? We leave that for some other writer somewhere else to dwell upon.

By the end of the 1860s organised rugby in England had become widespread, but without a central governing body arguments naturally cropped up between contesting clubs with their own ideas as to how the game should be conducted, not the least bone of contention being the legality of 'hacking', which many of the clubs wanted outlawed before death rather than mere serious injury started to enter into rugby. Soccer and rugby had become two distinctly different sports in 1863 with the formation of the Football Association and with the advent of the 1870s adherents of the handling code felt that the time had come for them to get their own house in order, with the establishment of a rugby union.

3. *The First Internationals*

I always like that story about the delegate who failed to turn up at the inaugural meeting of the Rugby Football Union because it is so typically rugby – or rugger, as they used to call it. (Whatever happened to 'rugger', that bit of schoolboy word coinage that came into being along with 'soccer'? Why should 'soccer' have persisted as a word in good standing, while 'rugger' is now outdated, to be used only in a jokey way, along with 'Twickers'?) The representative whom Wasps sent to that historic get-together in a London restaurant arrived instead at a pub of the same name and by the time it dawned on him that the other delegates probably hadn't turned up because they were meeting elsewhere it was too late to do anything but enjoy the local brew, thus welding the traditional link between rugby and beer.

Whether or not it is strictly accurate the fact remains that Wasps, though invited, were not there and so are now unable proudly to point to their being founder members of the R.F.U. Twenty-one other clubs were and the meeting was held on January 26, 1871, at the now non-existent Pall Mall Restaurant at No. 1 Cockspur Street on an island site adjoining Trafalgar Square where today stand a couple of banks and Canada House. Most of the founding clubs – with colourful names such as the Gipsies, Flamingoes, Hornets and Mohicans – are now defunct but eight of them are still thriving: Blackheath, Richmond, Civil Service, Guy's Hospital, Harlequins, St Paul's School, King's College and Wellington College. With three schools represented, one wonders why the most logical one of them all to be there was not invited but Rugby School was very much on hand in the form of Old Rugbeians who were the key men at the meeting.

If when deciding what to call their new sports society the thirty-two delegates had called it the *English* Rugby Football Union rather than merely the Rugby Football Union it would have avoided a lot of confusion that was to come among rugby writers around the world. But if they had done so it would have been inaccurate at the time, for the new body was open for any club in Britain to join, on payment of 5s. entrance and 5s. annual subscription, and indeed when Scottish clubs formed their own rugby union in 1873 it became necessary for them to sever their connection with the R.F.U.

At the meeting a Committee of thirteen was chosen, with Algernon Rutter, a solicitor who played in the forwards for Richmond, elected as first President of the R.F.U. Edwin H. Ash, of Richmond Military College and leading light in the formation of the Richmond club, became Hon. Secretary and Treasurer. And Rutter, with E. C. Holmes and L. J. Maton, were entrusted with the important task of drawing up the first code of Laws of the Rugby Football Union. All these gentlemen were Old Rugbeians.

Working whenever time permitted in the legal chambers of Holmes, the evolving of a unified set of rules for the game seemed like such a complicated and interminable job for the three lawmakers that it appeared doubtful whether they would ever get it done in time for approval at the first Annual General Meeting, set for October of that year, and for use in the new season. But fortunately, as it turned out, Leonard Maton broke a leg while playing for his club, Wimbledon Hornets, and incapacitated on a sofa and supplied by his two colleagues with all the tobacco he might need for his beloved pipe he had the leisure to concentrate on the Code. And so it came to be revealed in his obituary in the *Morning Post* when he died at the age of 88 in 1933 that it was entirely 'with his own hand' that the first set of 59 Rugby Union Laws were drawn up, to be approved by the committee on June 22, 1871, and accepted in their entirety by a general meeting of the R.F.U. specially called on June 24.

There was a Plan of the Field, which had the familiar rectangular look of a rugby pitch but that was all, merely touchlines and goal lines, no halfway, no 25s and – most important – no deadball line. 'Mauls in goal' were a great feature of the game in those early days and it seems that it was felt that no geographical restriction should be placed on where these could be conducted. Not until 1891 was a deadball line introduced, with a maximum of 25 yards. Measurements for the field of play were not specified; the now familiar 110 x 75 yards did not come until 1879. The only thing that the original Laws were specific about was the size of the goal posts, 18 ft. 6 in. apart and 10 ft. to the crossbar, which remains unchanged today. There was not even any stipulation as to number of players per team, presumably because at that time everybody knew that a rugby side consisted of 20 players.

Thirty of those 59 original Laws of rugby still have direct relevance today, in other words almost exactly half, provided you concede such things as 'throwing out' meaning throwing in from touch. Most of the laws that have fallen by the wayside are the ones concerned with those mauls in goal. Only those who actually had a hand on the ball could participate in those standing-up battles. Anyone who lost grip and attempted to rejoin the maul could legitimately be 'dragged out by the opposite side'. When at long last a member of the attacking team managed to make a touchdown he got no points for his side (Law 7: 'A match shall be decided only by a majority of goals.'). It merely allowed him to do a 'punt out', to the other members of his team in the field of play, the catcher being entitled to a kick at goal. This 'punt out' business, however, became so complicated and the rewritten rules regarding it so difficult to interpret that in 1883 it was scrapped in favour of the present procedure for a kick at goal from a try.

There was no mention of a referee, although it is known that prior to this the usual thing at Rugby School was to have two umpires. The R.F.U.'s first code merely stated, in Law 59: 'The captains of the respective sides shall be the sole arbiters of all disputes.' Which must have made for some interesting situations. In 1875 the R.F.U. ruled that umpires could be appointed if desired; if not 'the captains' decisions shall be final'. Six years later neutral umpires were appointed for all matches and in 1884 the International between Scotland and Wales was the first played in Britain with one referee and no umpires. In 1885 the referee got his whistle. It could well have been an idea borrowed from New Zealand because in May of the previous year a Canterbury sheep-farmer, W. H. Atack, went on record as saying: 'The referee had to use his voice to stop the game, and when both sides were appealing the voice had to be exercised loudly, and he found it exhausting. Thinking it over at home one day, my fingers strayed into a pocket where they encountered my dog whistle. The inspiration came to me that it would be a fine thing to use the whistle to stop the game. The next time I refereed I called the teams together and they agreed to play to the whistle. It was a great success and was speedily adopted all over the country.'

Thus were the original rules and regulations drawn up for the Rugby Football Union by the convalescent Mr Maton modified and augmented over the years until we have today the most convoluted set of Laws for any sport. The original code was ready for application in the 1871–72 season, lithographed copies of the Laws being distributed to the clubs at a total cost of 4 gns. This was revealed at the first annual general meeting of the R.F.U. at London's Arundel Hotel on October 25, 1871. The statement of accounts disclosed also that the Union's cash in hand was 11s. Now, of course, it is considerably more.

On November 19, 1870, a football match billed as between England and Scotland had taken place and it had infuriated many rugby followers, particularly those north of the Border. It was played under Association rules and not only did the result, a win for England, annoy the Scots rugby fans but they were quick to point out that it could not rightfully be called an International. All the so-called Scotland side had been drawn from London residents, for the simple reason that soccer as yet had made little impact in Scotland, where the schools, academies and universities played rugby exclusively.

Shortly after this and before the R.F.U. actually came into being a group of irate Scottish rugbymen (mainly of Edinburgh Academy, Edinburgh Academicals, Merchistonians, St Andrew's University and West of Scotland) issued a challenge to England for a more fully representative football match between the two countries. Some English club players formed a committee, headed by Frederic Stokes, captain of Blackheath, to accept this challenge and by the time the R.F.U. was formed on January 26, 1871, the new governing body was able to push through the arranging of the fixture, to take place at the ground of Edinburgh Academy, at Raeburn Place, on Monday, March 27, 1871.

The England XX for rugby's first ever International was:

Backs: A. Lyon (Liverpool), A. G. Guillemard (West Kent) and R. R. Osborne (Manchester);
Three-quarter back: W. MacLaren (Manchester);
Half-backs: F. Tobin (Liverpool), J. E. Bentley (Gipsies) and J. F. Green (West Kent);
Forwards: F. Stokes (Capt.), C. W. Sherrard, B. H. Burns and C. A. Crompton (Blackheath), A. Davenport and J. M. Dugdale (Ravenscourt Park), A. S. Gibson and H. J. C. Turner (Manchester), R. H. Birkett (Clapham Rovers), J. H. Luscombe (Gipsies), A. St G. Hamersley (Marlborough Nomads), J. H. Clayton (Liverpool) and D. P. Turner (Richmond).

Exactly half the side were Old Rugbeians, which seemed fitting. Stokes, the organiser and leader, was to become the second and youngest ever (at 24) President of the R.F.U. He played cricket for Kent and got near enough to being a double International with several appearances for the Gentlemen. He was one of England's earliest top class golfers. R. H. Birkett *was* a double International, with the rare distinction of having turned out for England at both rugby and soccer, plus being the first player ever to score a try for his country. A. G. Guillemard had a distinguished career as rugby administrator, going up through Secretary, Treasurer to President of the R.F.U. and much is owed to him by later rugby historians for his illuminating writings on the game in its early days. A. St G. Hamersley, a product of Marlborough, was to migrate to New Zealand where, as captain of the Christchurch club, he had much to do with the early popularising of rugby out there and then when he went on to Canada in the 1880s played the same sort of role as founder and first chairman of the British Columbia Rugby Union.

There is no interesting little story behind how the England side came to be the Men in White, as with how the Springboks got their particular colours. Up to 1903 South Africa always played in the colours of the provincial union which was staging a Test. But in 1903 in the pavilion at Newlands, Cape Town, when South Africa were about to play the British tourists the home captain, 'Fairy' Heatlie, found a set of jerseys of a local, defunct club and decided to fit his team out with them. They just happened to be green, looked good, and thenceforth became the regular South African strip. The springbok emblem – and the title 'Springboks' – came later, in 1906 when Paul Roos, captain of the first South African side to tour Britain, decided to add it to the erstwhile Old Diosecans' Club colours. England's white turnout, with red rose emblem, came into being purely and simply because the committee responsible for organising England's first rugby visit to Scotland decided that that was the way it would be, for future generations to emulate. The only radical difference then was that the players wore white knickerbockers, to be replaced by those delightful baggy shorts of pre-war days with pockets designed especially, it seemed, for ruggermen to put their hands into for trotting jauntily out on to the field on parky winter afternoons, until eventually today we have the abbreviated shorts brought literally to a high point by Andy Ripley, whose crotch-clutching version are reminiscent of those of skinny-legged French schoolboys.

The pioneering England XX went up by train overnight to Edinburgh, travelling third class on bare board seats (each paid all his own expenses) and arriving at dawn on the day of the match – hardly the best of preparation for the game which was to be 50 minutes each way.

The weather was fine and a surprisingly good crowd of 4,000 was on hand to watch what was described afterwards as 'a titanic struggle'. As mentioned earlier, the first official Laws of Rugby had not specified measurements for the field of play, so that in this case the visitors found themselves playing on a pitch that measured 120 x 55 yards. One can only imagine how cluttered it was with 40 men milling around on a ground only as wide as today's distance between the goal line and halfway. Though not necessarily intentional, making it that narrow was to the advantage of the home side, the free-running backs for which English rugby was already noted finding themseleves constricted but not so the burly Scottish forwards, rugged then as now.

The first half was evenly fought, the verb being chosen advisedly in view of the stress placed on the maul in the rugby of those days. But shortly after the restart the Scots scored a goal which was to be long contested and was a contributing factor to the setting up of the International Board, whose only function at first was to settle such disputes.

What happened was that after a maul just outside the England goal line the umpires ordered the balll to be put down for a five-yard scrummage. But instead of grounding the ball the Scottish forwards mauled it over, touched down and claimed a try. Illegal according to the English reading of the Laws, it was nevertheless allowed and afterwards one of the umpires, H. H. Almond, a noted headmaster of Loretto, gave this splendid explanation: 'When an umpire is in doubt, I think he is justified in deciding against the side which makes the most noise. They are probably in the wrong.' W. Cross, of Glasgow Academicals, kicked the goal and, kicks at goal being the only means of scoring, Scotland were ahead 1–0.

England put the pressure on and R. H. Birkett, father of the great J. G. G. Birkett, who for a long time held the record of 21 appearances for England set up in 1912, did his 'run in' to secure England's first ever try. It was close to touch and the versatile Stokes, outstanding place-kicker as well as all his other ball playing achievements, was not able to cope with this one because of a strong cross-wind. Still 1–0 to Scotland. The Scots got another try, also not turned into a goal, and that was the final score.

The England side, greeted by their supporters on their

return to Euston, told them that 'We were robbed' or whatever the 1871 equivalent was and no time was lost in arranging a revenge fixture for the following season. This was staged at the Kennington Oval on February 5, 1872 and was played at the top end of the ground where the Vauxhall Stand is now. Again the day was fine and again the crowd 4,000 which although all right for Edinburgh was disappointing for London, especially as this was indeed a needle match.

The touch and goal lines, merely 'cut out of the turf' in those days before white lines came into vogue, were of different dimensions from those of Raeburn Place, especially in the all-important aspect of width – 120 yards long by 70 wide, as against the skinny 55 in Scotland. The extra 15 yards was very much to the advantage of England's fleet of foot backs and they ran out comfortable winners, 2 goals and 2 tries to 1 goal.

The England-Scotland clash was then to become a regular annual fixture, the seed from which sprang the International Championship as we know it today, while also retaining its own special appeal with what came to be termed 'the Calcutta Cup match'. The Calcutta Cup came into being as the result of some Old Rugbeians, resident in that city, becoming embued in 1872 with the idea of setting up a rugby club, which was not far short of being the equivalent of trying to start a cricket club in Siberia. Naturally it was doomed to failure. Not only were the rock hard grounds so abrasive as to make the playing of rugby an agony but there was a dire shortage of opponents. Indians, noted in cricket for their batting characteristic of withdrawing several yards towards square leg when confronted with a bowler of anything above medium pace, were hardly likely to take to a game in which rugged bodily contact is a without-which-not. So for opponents the Calcutta club had to rustle up any cluster of whites available to form themselves into a rugby team – the Volunteers, Merchants and Brokers, the Griffs (Anglo-Indian for newly arrived Europeans).

In 1873 the arrival in India for a tour of duty of the 3rd Buffs, if not indeed rugby buffs, gave a fillip to the club's fixture list but when the regiment left in 1876 it was the swansong of the Calcutta F.C. and in the following year they ground to a halt. Oddly enough they had money in the bank. Being dedicated rugbymen, the general feeling was that they should hold a wake, main feature of which would be to blue the funds in a giant pissup. But more sober minds prevailed, in the form of the founder, captain, secretary and treasurer of the club – G. A. J. Rothney by name. He suggested something more lasting – the presentation of a trophy of Indian workmanship to the Rugby Union which would keep alive the memory of the gallant effort to make rugby take root in the unco-operative soil of Calcutta.

Letters were exchanged and eventually, in 1878, the R.F.U. were pleased to take possession of 'an international challenge cup to be played for annually by England and Scotland'. Although not the most attractive cup in the world, the 18 in. high trophy does have the merit of being very much out of the ordinary. In beaten silver, with snakes for handles and a miniature elephant for a grip on the potlid, it literally consists of the Calcutta club's cash in hand at the time of its demise. They took the money out of the bank in rupees and these were given to the craftsmen to melt down and fashion into the trophy.

It was a great idea, but there is something sorely amiss about the Calcutta Cup. We never see the confounded thing.

When the Queen takes time off from her beloved horse racing to give a nod to another sport, she is seen to present the F.A. cup after the Final and it is paraded round Wembley for all the fans to get a look at. Wimbledon's trophies are seen to be presented and held aloft. Horse of the Year cups are waved around in the breeze. The Greyhound Derby trophy is on display throughout the proceedings, with a special spotlight focused on it. Even cricket's Ashes, if not presented publicly, are on permanent view for anyone to see, in the museum behind the pavilion at Lords.

But not the Calcutta Cup, and one must admonish the Rugby Football Union for being slightly stuffy in this regard. How much more charisma would the annual event have if it were publicly presented after each match. But no. What happens is that it sits throughout the year in the vaults of London jewellers Longman and Strongitharm Ltd., only to be brought out and put on display in their window for the week preceding the England-Scotland game. There is a ceremony of sorts after the match. The two teams, in the secrecy of the dressing rooms, pass it around as a loving cup.

The only chance the rugby fans of seeing it is if you happen to be passing the jewellers, at 13 Dover Street, London W.1., in that pre-match week. And thereby hangs a tale . . .

It seems that the late Bernard Sunley, famed property man, had been approached by the leader of a boy scout group in the area where he lived and asked whether he would present them with a trophy for their annual tenting competition. It just so happened that he *was* passing No. 13, Dover Street, London W.1., during the week preceding an England-Scotland match and the cup caught his eyes. No rugby fan he, when he went into the shop under the impression that it was merely an article for sale on display in the window he did not take kindly to being told that he couldn't buy it. As a matter of fact it was with some heat that he informed the man behind the counter that he was not in the habit of meeting with refusal when he wanted to buy something. And it was only after his take-over bid for the Calcutta Cup had gone into four figures that the manager was called to convince him it wasn't for sale and he stomped out of the shop.

With Internationals between England and Scotland firmly established as an annual event, one might have thought that Wales would have been the next to join in. But as mentioned earlier, public schools and universities being the nursery of rugby and Wales being a bit short of these, the principality lagged behind in getting up to International level. In Ireland the universities and medical schools had taken enthusiastically to the game (over the years Dublin University has provided far and away the most Irish caps) and it was they who were next on the international scene.

England invited them over in 1875 and since there was no Irish Rugby Union (until 1879) the governing bodies of the south and the north agreed to send a XX to the Oval on February 19, each providing ten players, which in the event did not make for a good combination in view of the fact that each contingent were complete strangers to the other. The 3,000 spectators (who paid 1s. if on foot, 5s. for carriages and 10s. for omnibuses) saw a colourful team take the field, the white jerseys and long white trousers tucked into socks being brightened by strips of green. They were no match for England, however, Although good in the tight they had little idea of open play and in the essential department of kicks at goal were quite hopeless. The Englishmen could have scored at will but let them down lightly with a win of 2 goals and a try to nil.

The return match, which was to presage a regular annual fixture, was played on the Leinster cricket ground at Rathmines on December 13, 1875, and Ireland had clearly learned a lesson or two about kicking. It was a much more even game, won by England by a goal and a try to nil.

The match, played in the quagmire of a thaw after a heavy frost, was enlivened by a typical touch of the Irish flair now recognised as a characteristic of their game. The Dublin University three-quarter A. P. Cronyn received the ball in his own 25 and in evading tacklers had his jersey torn off. Stripped to the waist he dodged and weaved to within a yard of the England goal line before eventually being brought down, the delighted Dublin spectators admitted afterwards that his slippery body had much to do with his getting out of tackles on the way.

The popular demand for more open play – not necessarily stripped to the waist – saw the change in the following season from XXs to XVs and then after Wales had formed their Rugby Union in March, 1880, they made their belated entry into the International field, exactly a decade after the senior form of rugby had been launched. It was not an auspicious debut at the Blackheath ground on February 19, 1881, England slaughtering them to the tune of 7 goals, a dropped goal and 6 tries to nil, the Welsh line being crossed no fewer than thirteen times.

Another decade was to pass before Wales managed to achieve their first ever win over England but by then they had really applied themselves, including their introduction in 1886 of the four three-quarter system, which the other Home Countries followed, thus giving rise to the oft repeated lamentation, 'What was need are a couple of good centres', something from which Wales the innovators seldom seem to have suffered, what with Gwynn Nicholls & Gould, Bleddyn Williams & Matthews, etc.

Wales came to be very good at the game, as well we know now, and a basic reason why they did was because, as with those other great rugby countries, New Zealand and South Africa, it developed as a sport for the working class, who have an inclination to want to win rather than the less earnest approach of the public school and university rugbymen. The outcome was that despite Scotland being England's first and 'traditional' rivals the Big One as far as England was concerned became their annual clash with Wales, the one Home International that consistently packs Twickenham to capacity.

And so, when the turn of the century was reached, the International Championship was well under way in the British Isles, with only France to come and in 1910 make the tournament a five nations affair.

4. Clubland

Club rugby in England developed on precisely the same lines as soccer. That is to say that a London club, for example, would not only play the other local clubs but also go up to the Midlands and the North and elsewhere in England, and even venture into Wales.

But there the similarity ended, for two basic reasons.

First, the soccermen decided that theirs would be a money game. Rugby is the only major team sport (is hockey a major sport?) that has remained strictly amateur and that is something for which the youth of the land in particular can be everlastingly thankful.

If you're a youngster growing up in England and you are keen on sport you are faced with an awful dilemma when you leave school. If you are an enthusiast for soccer, say, or cricket and have dreams of playing for England there is only one way in which you can set about fulfilling that ambition. You have to become a full-time soccer player or cricketer. You have to get yourself signed up by Aston Villa or whatever, or become a net boy at Lord's or one of the other cricket headquarters. But that isn't necessarily what you want to do. You may want to embark on a career more lasting then sport, where you know your playing days have to finish in your late 30s, when you're in the prime of life in other jobs such as business, industry and the professions.

The answer, of course, is rugby – the only big-time sport in England which provides you with the best of both worlds. You can have your moments of glory playing for England (if you make it!) while at the same time furthering your career in banking, engineering, law or whatever it is you want to make good at. No dread hanging over you, as in soccer or cricket, that when you are 36, say, you have to find a new career for yourself and are likely to wind up in the downbeat situation of becoming Manager and Coach of the Pissville Hornets or a flag-showing rep for a brewery firm.

And of course the other difference of development between club rugby and club soccer was that the latter became competitive and organised itself into leagues. It is a great pity, we realise now, that English club rugby didn't do likewise.

The rugger diehards might raise their hands in horror at that. But it is true. The new generation of young rugbymen in this country desperately want Saturday-to-Saturday competitive rugby and they'll get it, but it is the devil's own job getting it organised, so entrenched is the more than 100-years-old system of clubs only playing friendlies each week.

The hold-out by the reactionaries of the R.F.U. against competitive club rugby was inconsistent. There has been an official county championship since 1889. If a competition between the clubs was 'not in the true spirit of the game', why was it acceptable at county level?

At the start of the 1970s, as a concession to the clamour of the more progressive rugbymen, the R.F.U. announced a national club knock-out competition. But it was not really what the progressives wanted. Their argument was that to improve club interest for both players and spectators and in the long term to raise the general standard of play there should be a system similar to that which had always been in use in South Africa and New Zealand – clubs playing in week-by-week competition in regional groups. In that way each match each Saturday would have some real meaning – each team striving to improve its place in the championship table. Then, it you like, have a knock-out competition between the winners of each regional championship, for added interest. But to introduce a mere knock-out, lacking as it does continuity of competition, would serve no real purpose as far as raising the standard of club rugby was concerned.

However, the R.F.U. persevered with their knock-out plans

and the first competition was played in the 1971–72 season. There was complete confusion as to how teams qualified, weird regulations such as that whereby a team that drew at home lost, a mish-mash of fixtures as the clubs tried to fit the knock-out in among long-standing arrangements, and wholehearted disinterest from the general public.

If the R.F.U. had anticipated that rugby's knock-out competition would take on some of the aura of the F.A. Cup, their hopes were either sadly misplaced or premature. It was hoped that all would come right in the end.

One would have thought that there was an easy, readily at hand way of improving the general standard of English rugby – developing the County Championship.

It is surprising that a competition that dates back to the 1880s does not loom more large on the rugby scene. There is keen interest in certain parts of the country and down in the West Country, for example, they are known to get wildly enthusiastic. But around the London area, with the great potential for big gates, there is an offhand attitude about the whole thing. Until the Mallaby Report county matches were sloughed off as mid-week fixtures and if you paid your first visit to a Middlesex v. Surrey match you would definitely be disappointed if you expected a huge crowd and all the excitement and general flim-flam of what, on paper, is a London 'derby'. In truth it's a case of if you brought your dog with you, you boosted the attendance considerably.

It is ironic that it is those big clubs who want competitive rugby who are the ones that militate against the competition that is already in existence being an excitedly followed series of matches, through the reluctance to part with good Saturday dates on their fixture lists and unwillingness to release key players for county service.

The clubs have built themselves up into the dominant part of the structure of English rugby. It is not the same in New Zealand and South Africa. There the clubs are merely local affairs. They don't go wandering all over the countryside. It is the provincial sides who do that. The clubs around Auckland, say, or Wellington merely play among themselves in a competition for a championship. (I avoid the word 'league' because of the obvious confusion with that other awful game Rugby League. But they are in fact leagues, although never referred to locally as such – merely 'the championship'.) From these club teams the provincial side is chosen and this might be as good a time as any to clear up the misunderstanding in many English minds. Although called provincial teams, that is a misnomer. They are in truth much more akin in area represented to county teams. When the Lions play Auckland, for example, they don't play the *province* of Auckland. They play a team which is drawn only from clubs in the region of the *city* of Auckland. The province that bears that name is broken up into at least half a dozen 'provincial teams', all of which have sufficient status to play the Lions on their own – Waikato, North Auckland, King Country, etc. And this applies to all the other large provinces.

As rugby grew up in New Zealand and South Africa on this basis – club locally, provincial nationally – the standard of rugby naturally rose. The English system of players playing most of the season at club level naturally held the game back and made it a poorly attended sport, except when raised to international level, i.e. the International and the matches against the big touring sides from overseas.

It really is a pretty poor show that apart from Twickenham there is no other really big, well appointed rugby ground in England, whereas New Zealand and South Africa each have a batch vastly superior to anything in this country outside the London H.Q.

And now let us be mercenary for a moment. (And why not be mercenary, since gate money in rugby is ploughed back into the game, not put into directors' pockets?) Another very good aspect of the importance of provincial rugby in New Zealand and South Africa is that by drawing far bigger crowds than club rugby there or in this country, the money comes pouring in.

The big grounds where Test Matches are played in New Zealand and South Africa were not built and controlled by the national Rugby Union as in Britain, with Twickenham, the Welsh National Stadium, Murrayfield and Lansdowne Road. In New Zealand, Auckland's Eden Park, Wellington's

Athletic Park, etc., and in South Africa, Johannesburg's Ellis Park, Cape Town's Newlands, etc., are merely local provincial grounds, built and controlled by the Auckland R.F.U., and Wellington R.F.U., etc. And where did they get the money to make them such big, well-appointed stadiums? Basically from provincial rugby.

Over the years if a provincial team in New Zealand had a good run with the Ranfurly Shield or in South Africa in the Currie Cup more and more fans turned up paying more and more money which in turn meant that larger accommodation was needed to cope with them and thus a happy spiral was built up. Out there provincial rugby was a money-spinner. In England county rugby never has been. Club rugby being the big thing in Saturday-to-Saturday rugby in this country it is just not possible to pull in enough revenue from the relatively small crowds to build bigger and better accommodation. It isn't really needed, anyway, is it? Except on those occasions when a club ground is used for a fixture involving one of the big overseas touring sides.

Someone once said that any sport gets the stadiums it deserves. The sport of club rugby has the small grounds its following warrants. International rugby has the magnificent Twickenham. The descent from Twickenham to the average club ground is like the difference between a Rolls-Royce and my five-year-old Imp.

5. *They Used to Call it 'Twickers'*

If a country is going to have a national rugby ground, it might as well be the best in the world. Which Twickenham is.

Welshmen will at once say, 'You just wait until the rebuilding of Cardiff Arms Park is finished!' At this time of writing, we are still waiting. Scotsmen will say that Murrayfield is much bigger. Quite right. Murrayfield accommodates far more people in discomfort than Twickenham does.

On behalf of the overseas rivals I would put in a brief for Eden Park, Auckland, on the basis that the ground that is the focal point of your rugby interest when you are growing up is naturally much better than the others. Venue of my rugby youth was then just one big wooden stand with a smaller, also wooden, one beside it, a bit of terracing opposite it and nothing else except the 'Scotsmen's grandstands' erected in the back gardens of the houses overlooking the ground from behind the terraces. Today Eden Park is a magnificent ground, with two huge modern stands and really first-class facilities as to changing rooms, etc. But there is one basic thing wrong with Eden Park and in which respect it can't hold a candle to Twickenham. It also does service as a cricket ground, with the result that even if you are in the best seats you are miles away from the rugby playing area, or more accurately over 40 yards from the nearest touchline, compared to the feeling at Twickenham that you can practically reach out and touch the players.

And an interesting sidelight to this is that I remember Don Rutherford telling me that the intimacy of Twickenham is a great advantage to a full-back. When you're kicking for touch at Eden Park, Johannesburg's Ellis Park and those others that double as cricket grounds you can be a bit adrift because you can't precisely pinpoint the bit of touchline away ahead of you where you hope to achieve a wonderful bit of touch-finding. It's like in cricket when you're trying to hit a six. How much easier it is to have trees or a fence edging the boundary line to aim at, rather than trying to gauge where a white line on open ground is. At Twickenham the accommodation coming right to the edge of the field provides a very helpful target.

In 1907 Twickenham was a market garden and it was in that year that the Rugby Union decided that they really must have a ground of their own, rather than holding their Internationals at Blackheath, Richmond and Leicester, which were at that time the venues they were using. Also their offices in Surrey Street, off the Strand, were proving inadequate and they needed something more fitting for a headquarters. So the site was bought and after two years' work on preparing the field and building an 'A' and 'B' stand on each side, plus terracing at the ends, the first match at Twickenham was played on October 2, 1909. It was between Harlequins and Richmond, Harlequins having taken the opportunity to become club tenants, after having been at Hampstead, Chiswick, Wimbledon and elsewhere.

Twickenham as an International ground had an auspicious opening with the long delayed victory over Wales on January 15, 1910. From a crowd of 18,000 the R.F.U. realised a profit of £2,000, a figure to be very pleased about in those days when a pound was really a pound. For comparison, a capacity crowd at Twickenham today is worth £100,000 . . . or I should say 'at time of writing', since by the time this appears the devaluation of the pound will probably mean that the Twickenham gate has reached a new record figure, just as each year this film or that play breaks all-time records for takings purely and simply because the price of seats has sky-rocketed.

Youthful rugby fans will probably be interested to know that Twickenham used to be referred to, seriously, as

Twickers, although they have no doubt heard it called that by someone poking fun at the old-timers. Twickenham being called Twickers, along with W. W. Wakefield being known affectionately as Wakers, etc., was an outgrowth of the slang of the people between the wars who were known as the Bright Young Things. In a nutshell, the way they used to talk: 'She got loaded on *champers*, ran around *starkers* and wound up *preggers.*'

As far as attendance is concerned, Twickenham has gone from strength to strength. From that original Wales match, this is how the record crowds have swelled:

1910:	18,000	for	England v. Wales
1913:	29,000	v.	South Africa
1924:	43,000	v.	Scotland
1936:	73,000	v.	New Zealand
1950:	75,157	v.	Wales

That 1950 record must unfortunately still stand for a while yet. I say unfortunately because it is not really the fault of the R.F.U. that that figure could now easily be passed but hasn't been. For two reasons. In the first place the police ruled that for comfort and safety there should be a crowd limit of 72,500, which at present is officially regarded as capacity at Twickenham. It is made up in this way:

West Stand:	12,000	(6,500 Lower, 5,500 Upper)
East Stand:	12,000	(6,500 Lower, 5,500 Upper)
North Stand:	3,500	(Upper)
Ringside:	5,000	(seated)
Standing:	40,000	(North Lower, West and East enclosures, South Terrace

Secondly, for some time now the Rugby Union has had plans all drawn up for a double-decker stand to replace the South Terrace and bring the capacity to 80,000. But unfortunately they ran into a snag. They own (for the use of the Secretary and other officials) some but not all of the row of houses behind the South Terrace. The stand is designed to be 90 ft. high and for the non-R.F.U. householders this runs foul of Ancient Lights, so development has to be postponed until such time as the Rugby Union can get possession of all the properties and not only build the new stand but also carry out something else for which the blueprints are ready. The entrance to Twickenham is the only thing about it that isn't impressive, being a series of little alleyways in between the houses. That will be changed, when planning permission is granted, to something much more worthy.

When the South Stand *is* built it will be just 2 ft. 10½ in. short of the highest point at Twickenham – the top of the West Stand. No place for anyone who suffers from vertigo, the upper deck of the West Stand, or for that matter the upper deck of the East. But as nothing compared to the Millard Stand at Athletic Park, Wellington. The 92 ft. 10½ in. of the West Stand is to the apex of the roof. In the roofless Millard Stand spectators in the back row watch the game from 110 ft. up!

Very much alive to the link between rugby and beer, the R.F.U. have made the lavatories at Twickenham commodious. The facilities in regard to this crowd-pleasing aspect are in fact better than at any other sports arena in Britain. Most certainly better than at Cardiff Arms Park, where one is reminded of the story of the Englishman visiting Paris who asked a gendarme where he could go. With a broad sweep of the arm the policeman replied: 'M'sieu, you have all of France.' One feels that the Welsh rugby fans, tanked up prior to an International at the Queen's, the Royal and neighbouring pubs, feel that they have the whole of their National Stadium.

As everybody who has been at Twickenham when the Queen is there knows, the Royal Box is an enclosure at the front of the committee accommodation in the plumb seats on the halfway line in the West Stand. But what is not generally known is that there is a little staircase that leads down from this box to a retiring room for sole use of Her Majesty. It contains easy chairs, a marble-topped dressing table with large wall mirrors, wash basins and two toilets. The Queen has never used it. One summer's day I was fortunate enough to be taken on a conducted tour behind the scenes at Twickenham and when we came to this retiring room naturally where the Queen has not been I went.

It is not only the Queen, of course, who is to be seen in

the Royal Box. One of the most memorable visits was that of Princess Alexandra for the air victims' charity match between England and France late in the 1973–74 season. It was marked by a splendid streak across midfield at half time, a policeman using his helmet to shield the full frontal of the captured streaker from Her Royal Highness's gaze. It topped Sid Going's changing of his shorts out in the open in front of the Royal Box to reveal bright red briefs during the All Blacks' tour in the previous season and gave rise to the biggest spontaneous burst of laughter ever heard at Twickenham.

The turf at Twickenham, rivalled for lush vivid green only by Lansdowne Road, is not necessarily the best surface in the world upon which to play rugby – according to players in the touring teams from overseas. Granted there is never any mud at Twickenham, not real mud as encountered in the quagmire that Sydney Cricket Ground can often be and the sort of thing one finds at New Zealand Test grounds when the rains come. But the basic reason is that luxuriant grass, not played on week after week and kept long by the standards of New Zealand and South Africa. All Blacks and Springboks constantly complain that the sacred Twickenham turf, on which they are not allowed to practice prior to a match, seems to them like trying to run around on a huge spring mattress. And their goal-kickers, not warned that parting the grass to make an avenue for the foot coming to the ball is a good idea, can find themselves dragging their studs through the turf and muffing shots until they get wise to it. The inference is that the Twickenham playing surface, familiar to the England players, is an advantage to them. However, statistics don't seem to bear that out, as indicated in the chapter 'England Against the Visitors' in which is detailed the sad record the home country always had against the tourists at Twickenham.

Twickenham's scoreboards, apart from telling you which team is leading and by how many points, are pretty hopeless. The only breakdown of points for each side consists of GOALS and TRIES. Since there are four ways of scoring a goal (a goal from a try, penalty goal, dropped goal and goal from a mark), the scoreboards are almost completely uninformative, especially in these days of high-scoring matches when it is absolutely impossible to figure out from the sparse information put up on the boards how precisely each side's score has been built up. However, this is a failing of each of the home International grounds. Perhaps some day at one of them a fully informative scoreboard will be pioneered.

The pressbox is spacious and very well appointed as to telephones, writing desks, washroom and private bar-buffet but does have the drawback of being in the East Stand, so that if one of the reporters wants an interview with players or officials after the match it is a long haul around to the West Stand where all that sort of thing is available.

Twickenham is far and away the most sociable of Britain's International grounds. None of the others have the tea rooms so popular as rendezvous after the match, where everybody launches into discussions about the game with whoever else happens to be at the same table, whether strangers or not. And Twickenham is the only one of the four big grounds at which there are bars open to the public. And what bars they are! Although I haven't actually paced it out I would say that on a stroll around the ground you can't walk more than 40 yards without encountering one. Inside it is an amiable rugby maul trying to get a drink and there is only one place more jam-packed – the next natural port of call.

Nothing much has changed at Twickenham since the 1930s when the last bit of major construction was done there (the erection of the double-decker West Stand in 1931). Granted there are now advertisements to be seen – but only on the east side of the ground, so that they get full display in front of the West Stand TV cameras of the B.B.C., who have exclusive coverage of matches at Twickenham and, according to their Charter, do not carry advertising on their screens. But going to Twickenham still means, for the majority of fans, being carried along amid the sea of people trooping up from the station, shoulder to shoulder across the entire width of the Whitton Road . . . past the foul-smelling hotdogs stands and the ticket touts being furious when they see someone selling a spare ticket at face value to a stranger . . . the unofficial programme sellers and the suckers who buy them finding out all too late just how unofficial they are . . . inside the ground the two distinctly different types with a common interest – the good old-fashioned Twickers fraternity (the men in sheepskin jackets, their wives with steamer rugs over their arms and sons in their public school going-out suits) and the sloppily dressed enthusiastic young rugby club types, laden with party-size cans of the beer making their way to the terraces . . . the playing of the National Anthem mercifully uninterrupted by Welsh nationalists as at Cardiff . . . and as the game gets under way the rather sedate cheering, low in decibel count compared to the un-English way the crowds of other rugby countries give voice . . . to the tea rooms for post mortems afterwards (if you're family) or into the bars (if you're on the loose with the boys) . . . then packed solid in the rugby specials back to Waterloo, glum if the scoreline has gone in favour of the opposition and an excited babble of rehashing the moments of glory if England has recorded a famous victory.

Most Exciting International Match: Barbarians v. All Blacks, December 16, 1967. This game, diverted from Cardiff Arms Park because of rebuilding there, was virtually the Lions v. New Zealand since the best available British Isles team was put in the field in the effort to end, in their final match, the tourists' unbeaten record. Played wide open at breakneck speed it proved so exciting that even the rugby writers in the pressbox were constantly on their feet, clapping, cheering and pounding their desks, thus throwing overboard and convention that in the pressbox everyone remains impartial. And when the clock showed that time was up all who were there, save the little contingent of New Zealand supporters, were ecstatic that the Baa-Baas had pulled it off, the game was theirs, 6–3. But . . . there was a bit of injury time to be added on. And the All Blacks scored, to make it a draw, 6–6. And scored again in the fourth and final minute of extra time – to snatch the match away from the Britishers, 11–6.

Most Spectacular Debut for England: Richard Sharp in the Wales match, 1960. In the previous season the man in possession of the fly-half slot for England had been Bev Risman. He was naturally picked for the game against Wales in this new season but on the night before he had to pull out with flu – one of the most unfortunate flu bugs that ever hit a rugby player, as far as he was concerned. A promising young stand-off named R. A. W. Sharp, who had impressed for Oxford and Bristol, got a hurry-up call to Twickenham for his first cap. He sliced Wales to ribbons, scything through their backs time and again in such spectacular fashion that it was his presence alone in the side that brought England, with their 14–6 victory, their best win over the Welsh for twenty years. No wonder that henceforth the job was his. Poor Risman, following a couple of games after that at centre, had to turn to Rugby League.

Most Depressing Moment: Arriving at Twickenham for the opening match of the 1967–70 Springboks' 'demo' tour, against Oxford, to find the place converted into what to all intents looked like a prison camp.

Biggest Laugh: That streaker who entertained Princess Alexandra and the rest of the big crowd right royally at half-time of the England-France charity match in 1974.

Best Individual Try: Richard Sharp in the Scotland match in 1963. From near halfway on the right hand side of the field he was given possession from a scrum. He dummied the breakaways. He dummied the centres and as if by magic found his way through the narrow gap between them. And then when confronted by the Scots full-back he threw him a massive dummy which Blaikie accepted with such enthusiasm that he was well on his way towards the man outside Sharp when he glided inside him to score at the left of the posts. One dummy to make a break is quite good but three of them in succession to pentrate in turn each of your opponents' three lines of defence – that was something really memorable.

Note: One might put forward two other great Twickenham tries as rivals to Sharp's for the title of best – Obolensky's second against New Zealand in 1936 and Andy Hancock's v. Scotland in 1965. However, Obolensky's try, which had covered virtually the same ground as Sharp's was a case of the Flying Prince seeing a wide gap in the defence and his speed taking him diagonally through it unmolested; it had not had the same brilliant outwitting of successive would-be tacklers of the Sharp try. Similarly, with Hancock. The touchline on his wing was vacant when he was given possession 95 yards out and he just ran and ran, his opposing full-back muffing the tackle through a bad take-off from the muddy pitch when the time came to challenge. So, on balance, I would say that the accolade goes to Richard Sharp, who incidentally would definitely have been accused of trying to do too much and without doubt would have been dropped from the England side for losing the match if his final dummy hadn't come off and he had thrown away a certain try!

Best Team Try: Waka Nathan's second try in the 1963–64 All Blacks' 27–0 win over London Counties. Held in check by a strong London pack in the first half, the tourists cut loose in the second, running in seven tries in all. And it was the last one which brought the entire crowd to their feet to applaud the All Blacks as they trooped back from the Counties' goal line, the most sustained standing ovation I have ever witnessed at Twickenham. There had never been such a team try in a major match – until eclipsed by that now famous one by the Barbarians *against* the All Blacks at Cardiff in 1973. The crowd-thriller in 1963 was initiated by All Black centre Paul Little who somehow managed to get possession from a line-out in the tourists' 25. He slipped a pass to Chris Laidlaw, who set off upfield and then, in the words of Andy Mulligan, 'the ball went like a coconut from hand to hand twice across the field'. Onlookers lost count of how many All Blacks handled in their criss-cross progress towards the Counties' line but everyone who was there remembers vividly the final touch, the ultimate humiliation of defenders quite at a loss to cope with what was going on – Whineray stooping forward and tossing the ball back between his legs for Nathan to do a high dive over the line with it.

Most Exciting Match-winner: Peter Jackson v. Australia in 1958. In what was probably the dirtiest International ever played at Twickenham, England and Australia were level at 3–3 as full time came up but the Aussies had inflicted so much damage on the England players (one of them off the field and three others wandering around concussed) that everyone knew there would be a fair bit of injury time. No one expected, however, that it would be no less than 12 minutes. And it was in that final twelfth minute that Peter Jackson, getting hold of a loose ball 30 yards out, sidestepped his way past the converging defence and with the classic dropping of his inside shoulder as he went for the corner being able to prevent himself from being tackled into touch as he made his dive for the line. Ear-splitting pandemonium from the crowd, who wanted to let it be known that justice had been done against a side which had taken the field apparently determined to short-arm, late-tackle and kick their opponents into submission.

Greatest Drop-kick: I was not there in 1932 to see Gerry Brand's huge 90-yarder for South Africa which is in the record books as the longest ever, on any ground. So my award would go to Bob Hiller, for two in one match, each from near halfway, against Ireland in 1970. Two beautiful skyscraping kicks which meant the winning margin in England's 9–3 victory.

6. *The Golden Era*

The International Championship of course doesn't officially exist, being merely something made up by the press to make the annual friendly Internationals more interesting. But official or not, England should by rights have dominated it from the outset and continued to do so for quite some time, being the original patentees of the invention of rugby and therefore with more experience and know-how than the other countries which took it up.

It was not the case, however, and the basic reason was what was to become known as the schism of 1893, which was to do grave damage to the game and from which England was not fully to recover until almost twenty years had passed. Having shared the Championship back and forth with Scotland up until 1892, England was not to win it again until 1910.

The crisis stemmed from the desire of the northern clubs, primarily those of Yorkshire and Lancashire, to pay their players for 'broken time' – compensation for wages lost. The game up there had been embraced with such enthusiasm that adherents were drawn not merely from those of Public School background, as in the south, and time off from work for rugby often as not meant being seriously out of pocket.

Things came to a head at a tense general meeting of the R.F.U. on September 20, 1893, when committee member J. A. Millar, of Yorkshire County, tabled a motion 'that players be allowed compensation for *bona fide* loss of time'. G. Rowland Hill, Honorary Secretary of the Union, promptly stepped in with an amendment: 'That this meeting, believing that the above principle is contrary to the true interest of the game and its spirit, declines to sanction the same.'

Hill had rallied around him support, notably from William Cail, a former President who although himself from the north was willing to help in the fight against the threat of professionalism. So vital was the issue that canvassers went around southern clubs collecting proxy votes from those not sending representatives to the meeting and the 120 proxies thus obtained formed an important part of the 282–136 majority which carried the amendment. Twenty-two Yorkshire and Lancashire clubs withdrew forthwith from the Union, to form what was initially called the Northern Union and what we now know as Rugby League.

Conscious that the northerners were not likely to let it go at that, the anti-pro bloc shortly afterwards called a special meeting with the object of formulating safeguards against further inroads into the true interest and spirit of the game. Bye-laws were passed stressing the entirely amateur nature of rugby and these were to form the framework of the first, extremely strict Rules as to Professionalism, passed at the General Meeting on September 19, 1895.

How thankful we are to George Raymond Hill, who earned in his time the title of the Grand Old Man of rugby, knighted in 1926 for his services to the game and commemorated by the Rowland Hill Memorial Gates one passes through approaching the West Stand at Twickenham. Without his wonderful efforts, rugby could well have become a pro sport and all we would have had today would have been that awful game Rugby League, something which doesn't even bear thinking about.

Just how important northern rugby was at the time is indicated by the fact that nine players from the north dominated the England side that had last won the Championship and in 1879 it had been deemed necessary to switch the venue of England's home Internationals from southern grounds to Manchester and Leeds because of the greater support up there. When the 22 Yorkshire and Lancashire clubs withdrew in 1893 (and England's Internationals not unnaturally returned south), the total R.F.U. affiliation was 481 clubs, with 80 other applications pending. In three years

David Duckham, one of the most outstanding players in English rugby in the 1970s, pictured here as he is challenged by Joe Karam during the England v. New Zealand match at Twickenham in 1972. *Below left:* Budge Rogers, at the time of writing second only to John Pullin in the number of caps won for England (34). Here he leads out the England team against France in February 1969. *Below right:* W. J. A. Davies, who won 22 caps for England between 1913 and 1923

The England team against New Zealand, 1925. *From left, back row:* A. E. Freethy, R. J. Hillard, J. S. Tucker, R. Hamilton-Wilkes, H. J. Kittermaster, J. L. Gibbs, V. G. Davies, A. T. Young, J. Brough. *Front row, from left:* R. Cove-Smith, A. F. Blakiston, A. T. Voyce, W. W. Wakefield (capt.) L. J. Corbett, G. S. Conway, R. Edwards. *Below:* The England team against Ireland, 1974. *From left, back row:* K. A. Pattinson (touch judge), P. J. Squires, A. Neary, P. J. Dixon, A. G. Ripley, C. W. Ralston, R. M. Uttley, F. E. Cotton, C. B. Stevens, D. J. Duckham, M. Joseph (referee). *Front row, from left:* D. Roughley, G. W. Evans, S. Smith, J. V. Pullin (capt.), A. G. B. Old, P. Rossborough

A maul in goal, a feature of rugby in the 19th century

A print showing a moment from the England v. Ireland game at Dublin in 1899

The home of English rugby. Twickenham packed for the England v. Wales match in January 1966. *Below:* A lineout during the University rugby match in 1910. In those days Oxford and Cambridge met at the Queen's Club for their annual fixture it had dropped to 383. Five years later it had reached a low of 244. Thirty years were to elapse before membership was to be restored to the 1893 level and take an upward swing.

Such a scar did the northern breakaway inflict on the face of English rugby that it was not surprising that the national side could not put in a good appearance for many years. The Golden Era did come, however, in the period 1913 to 1924, a time of England dominance of the International Championship which is often termed the 'Wakefield Era'. It is slightly unfair to call it that. W. W. Wakefield did indeed lead England to a high point of her rugby but much of the groundwork had been laid some years before, notably by forward Pillman and backs Stoop and Poulton-Palmer.

If in this chapter I may appear to be rather cursory in regard to the big names behind England's vintage period, the explanation is simple. They are to be found in the chapter devoted to the all-time greats of English rugby.

The lean years were brought to an end dramatically in 1910 with a resounding win against Wales, the first for a dozen years, in the first International at the newly opened Twickenham. Victories over Scotland and France and a draw with Ireland made England worthy champions, a welcome novelty after her eighteen years in the International wilderness.

The player usually given almost sole credit for this revival was Harlequin fly-half Adrian Stoop. Indeed much of the England success stemmed from his magnificent individual play. More than that. He was to set the style for English back play which has come through to us today. But to be a shining individualist, two things are essential – possession and support. Up front 'Cherry' Pillman, as much an innovator as regards forward play as Stoop was among the backs, must take his share of the credit for establishing the sort of forward domination which provided the ideal climate for Stoop to function in. And beside him Stoop had one of England's greatest ever centres – Ronnie Poulton-Palmer.

This triumph in the 1910 Internationals was the opening fanfare for a run of success that English rugby fans are still hoping will some day be repeated. Runners-up to Wales in

1911, England shared the title with Scotland in 1912 and then this was their great record:

1913: Grand Slam
1914: Grand Slam
– War –
1920: Joint Champions with Wales and Scotland
1921: Grand Slam
1922: Runners-up to Wales
1923: Grand Slam
1924: Grand Slam

Having never previously achieved the Triple Crown, they rectified that with a vengeance, each of their five outright titles in those seven seasons of their vintage years not only being accompanied by a Triple Crown but also the complete whitewash of the opposition. Of the 28 matches played in that period they lost only two and drew one – points for 392, points against 188.

Those early heroes of the English revival – Stoop, Poulton-Palmer and Pillman – had not been available to carry on after the war (Poulton-Palmer for the sad reason that he was killed) but the great winger C. N. 'Kid' Lowe straddled the war. A Dulwich and Cambridge product, he set up the still standing record of 25 consecutive caps and had it not been for the enforced lay-off he would surely have the record for England's most capped player. And another who played before and after the war was W. J. A. Davies, who took over the stand-off slot from Stoop in 1913 and was joined by C. A. Kershaw in 1920 to form England's greatest ever half-back combination and an integral part of her match-winning formula in the latter part of the Golden Era.

Chief architect, though, of the grandstand finish to the vintage years was of course W. W. 'Wakers' Wakefield, whom I must confess I never saw in action, apart from my watching him make an electioneering speech outside our house when we lived in Blenheim Road in the borough of St Marylebone when he was seeking to retain his seat in the House of Commons in the 1950s. I am sure that his reception at Twickenham was never, ever as sparse and lukewarm.

As pack leader and later captain he was the inspiration of

his forwards, and the cornerstone of the England success in the early 1920s was the domination they established up front. No matter how good your backs are, it is forward power that rules the roost, as so often demonstrated by the great All Black and Springbok sides. The fast-breaking back row, to spoil opponents' possession and to link with their own inside-backs on attack, is familiar enough to us now but it was Wakefield, with colleagues Tommy Voyce and the man who is now Sir Arthur Blakiston Bt., who first developed the technique. And to capitalise on the opportunities they made they had behind them a line of backs who were to play practically unchanged throughout the period – Kershaw and Davies, centres Ted Myers and A. M. Smallwood with the above mentioned Lowe on the wing. Result: a side which in the last seasons of their Golden Era were literally invincible.

It was inevitable that after her great run through the 1910s into the 1920s England should taper off. The 1930s were an undistinguished decade, enlived from time to time, however, with such things as two magnificent English performances against the giants from down below the equator. In 1931 the genuinely sensational win by Leicester Midlands against the otherwise unbeaten Springboks . . . in 1936 England's trouncing of the All Blacks . . . treated at justifiable length in the chapter England Against the Visitors.

There was rather a damper on the International Championship as a whole in the 1930s, following a resolution passed on February 13, 1931 by the Rugby Football Union Committee and endorsed by the other home Unions to the effect that: 'After examination of the documentary evidence furnished by the French Federation and the 14 dissentient clubs, we are compelled to state that, owing to the unsatisfactory condition of the game of Rubgy football as managed and played in France, neither our Union nor the clubs of the Union under its jurisdiction will be able to arrange or fulfil fixtures with France or French clubs, at home or away.' French rugby was in turmoil through incessant rough play, molesting of referees, poaching of players and other indications of professionalism, and all contact across the Channel was cut off until such time as they could put their house in order. (Forgiven in 1940, they were fully restored when World War II ended.)

The split meant that the Five-nations Championship became merely a four-horse race, dubbed the Home International Championship, and there was naturally a lessening of interest in the truncated fixture list, not to mention regret at the absence of the colour the volatile French always contributed to the tournament.

Those great regulars – Wakefield and Co. – who season after season had given England supporters so much to be proud about had all retired as the 1920s were coming to a close and in the 1930s no other players came on the scene, as a group, consistently to be the backbone of the England side.

Doug Prentice, the Leicester forward, might have been thought to be the man to take over the mantle of Wakefield. After all, he captained the popular Lions in Australia and New Zealand in 1930. But that appointment, at the age of 34, had been a diplomatic move. He had never been a particularly good player, having won only a grand total of three caps, in 1928. His rugby talents lay chiefly off the field. A selector from 1932 to 1947, he was a splendid Secretary of the R.F.U. from the latter year until 1962.

Centre Carl Aarvold, a star of that 1930 Lions tour, took over the England captaincy on his return and could have been the key man in a set of backs that would do outstanding, regular service for the country. But they didn't seem to be around.

Sobey and Spong, a combination of names that rolls nicely off the tongue, had been a sensational pair of schoolboy half-backs for Mill Hill, on the outskirts of London, in the 1920s – on a par with schoolboys Tanner and Davies who were to emerge in Wales shortly afterwards. Scrum-half Sobey and fly-half Spong came to maturity with Old Millhillians and when they made their debut together for England in 1930 and were at once picked for the Lions tour of that year, all seemed set for England to have, for years to come, a pair behind the scrum worthy of comparison with Kershaw and Davies. But sad to say Sobey was knocked out of the Lions tour in the first match and after that unhappy setback to their joint careers they never really got together again as an effective force in Internationals.

Peter Cranmer, Oxford and Moseley, 16 caps 1934–38, was a centre of class and a man of parts – captain of Warwickshire at cricket and BBC rugby commentator. In one of his two Varsity Matches he had behind him as full-back the South African Rhodes Scholar 'Tuppy' Owen-Smith and they were to share this association in Internationals, Owen-Smith being one of the best ever England – if not English – full-backs.

Prince Obolensky, the Flying Slav, whom we probe more deeply when on the subject of England Against the Visitors, had that one afternoon of greatness, which unfortunately he quite failed to live up to in the three Home Internationals in the same 1936 season and then disappeared from the International scene. Who would worry about that, though, when he left such an imprint on it? What was really sad, however, was that like another much talked about England three-quarter before him – Ronnie Poulton-Palmer – he was to be among those rugby Internationals who have died in uniform, as a Pilot Officer in the RAF.

Far and away the best forward in England in the 1930s was George Beamish, RAF and Leicester, 25 caps. Unfortunately his caps were for Ireland. England could have done with him. It was not a period of great English forwards.

H. B. Toft, RAF and Lancashire (captain and 64 appearances), 10 caps, was a good hooker and later a popular member of the pressbox as chief rugby writer for the *Observer.* But where were the forwards to follow with distinction in the tracks of Wakefield, Voyce, Conway, Blakiston? England would dearly have loved to have been able to borrow from Wales a forward of the time who had precisely the same sort of speed and flair in the loose – Ivor Jones.

And if it came to borrowing, the man whom perhaps they would most have liked to take over was a Scottish fly-half who was one of rugby's greatest stars of the 1930s – R. Wilson Shaw. He had humbled England at Twickenham in the 1938 Calcutta Cup match in what was regarded then as a high-scoring International – 21–16 to Scotland, with Wilson Shaw nailing down the lid with one of Twickenham's best tries in which, getting possession of a loose ball well out, he appeared to zig-zag his way through the entire England side.

And one thing certain, if England had been able to avail themselves of his services he would have been played always at fly-half, instead of his talents so often being wasted by experimenting with him at centre and wing as the Scottish selectors did.

7. *'The Public Schools Championship'*

I once did a magazine article called 'The Public Schools Championship', the idea being to arrive at which of the famous English schools were best at producing notable Old Boys in all fields of endeavour. There was a chart with categories listed along the top – politics, the Services, big business, the arts, sport, etc. Down the left the various schools were listed. Points were allocated for turning out a successful Old Boy – five for a Prime Minister, four for an outstanding Judge, three for a successful writer and so on. Down the right were the total points for each school. Eton breezed it, far outscoring any other school. (As a matter of interest, Winchester was second, Harrow third, followed by Westminster and Marlborough)

While researching this book it struck me that it mightn't be a bad idea to adapt this to rugby – which are the champion schools at producing England internationals?

One thing certain was that this was a championship that Eton was not going to dominate, for much the same reason that other great Public Schools such as Charterhouse, Lancing and Malvern would not be featuring on the list. Although not entirely a soccer school, it is only in recent years that rugby has taken on any sort of importance at Eton, in competition to soccer and their own Wall Game and Field Game. There has in fact been only one Etonian who has ever played rugby for England – Sir Isaac Pitman, with one solitary appearance against Scotland in 1922. Although better known for his association with shorthand, he was quite an athlete in his youth – Public Schools welter-weight boxing champion, a Triple Blue at Oxford (rugby, athletics and skiing).

I should mention that in undertaking the somewhat demanding task of going through the more than 1,000 names of those who have won England caps to find out where they had been to school it is highly probable that my figures in the list below are not 100 per cent accurate. I am sure that I shall get indignant letters from readers with specialised knowledge, i.e. Old Boys of some particular school who know precisely and quote with pride the number of their school's England caps. I apologise now for inaccuracies that may have crept in through my attempting to research *all* the 200-plus Public Schools, not just one. The point is that what has been aimed at is an over-all picture of which are indeed England's great rugby schools and an omission here and there will not change radically the broad scene.

It is a term one hears often – this or that revered seat of learning is 'a great rugby school'. What I find fascinating about the list – which I'm sure by now you've skipped ahead to have a look at – is that more than one of those constantly referred to as 'a great rugby school' haven't managed to make the top ten in the charts, as our friends in the world of pop music say. One might have thought Haileybury would have been higher and as for Oundle and Blundell's, each with but four caps, 'let's hope for a better showing next term' could well be the entry in their Report.

Most intriguing, I find, is the performance of Giggleswick, a school of merely 270 pupils near Settle in Yorkshire. What an achievement for them to have produced as many England caps as Harrow and more than such other giants as St Paul's, Winchester, Cranleigh and Whitgift.

If you're wondering about *your* school and where it stands . . . Stowe has produced but one cap but of course they are a young school which only came into being in the early 1920s and they can at least point with pride to the fact that one of their founder-pupils who used to lean against the First XV scrum was David Niven. Repton also has only one and likewise Shrewsbury and King's School, Canterbury, which makes me less unhappy about the fact that all my 400-years-old school has ever come up with was Mike Bulpitt.

The school which did dominate the list, logically, was Rugby and they proved to be as far ahead of the others as Eton had been in the general production of outstanding Old Boys. And there was an interesting parallel. The dominance of Old Etonians in most walks of life has much to do with the old pals' act or the old school tie circuit, whichever you want to call it. In Big Business, Law and so on there is a definite tendency for Old Etonians to look with favour on their kind and this applies especially to politics, where an Etonian Prime Minister can be fully expected to pack his cabinet with chums from the old school. (With Socialists it is quite different, of course. When Harold Wilson manages to get into power he is not known to fill his Cabinet with Wirral Grammar School old boys.)

The Etonian friendship league had its counterpart in rugby, with Old Rugbeians very much running the show when Internationals started at the beginning of the 1870s. So packed with young men from Rugby were the early England sides that it reached some sort of high-water mark of the old pals' act when a certain Dawson Palgrave Turner found himself being capped for England despite the fact that he had never been good enough to make the school team when at Rugby. When one remembers that in those days they played XXs and not merely XVs one can see that Rugby School was at once able to pile up a lead over other schools in the production of England caps that was so large that it is not now ever likely to be overtaken.

THE ENGLISH PUBLIC SCHOOLS CHAMPIONSHIP

	School	*No. of Old Boys Capped by England*	*Great Players*	*Period*
1.	Rugby	41	Adrian Stoop	1900s
			Ronnie Poulton-Palmer	1910s
			M. R. Steele-Bodger	1940s
2.	Marlborough	25	A. St G. Hamersley (in England's 1st Int.)	1870s
3.	Clifton	23	H. G. Periton (21 caps)	1920s

	School	*No. of Old Boys Capped by England*	*Great Players*	*Period*
4.	Cheltenham	22	R. L. Aston (Lions' greatest try scorer)	1890s
5.	Uppingham	20		
6.	Tonbridge	19	'Cherry' Pillman	1910s
			R. W. D. Marques (23 caps)	1950s
7.	Wellington	18	H. T. Gamlin	1900s
8.	Durham	12	Carl Aarvold	1920–30s
			Mike Weston (29 caps)	1960s
9.	Bedford	12	A. F. Blakiston	1920s
			Budge Rogers (34 caps)	1960s
10.	Merchant Taylors'	11	R. Cove-Smith (29 caps)	1920s
11.	Haileybury	10	J. G. G. Birkett (21 caps)	1900–1910s
12.	Sherborne	9		
13.	Mill Hill	7	W. H. Sobey & R. S. Spong	1930s
	Dulwich	7	C. N. Lowe (25 caps)	1910s
15.	Giggleswick	6		
	Harrow	6		

After this there is a batch of schools each with around four caps, including: St Paul's, Cranleigh, Oundle, Whitgift, Blundell's, Winchester, King Edward's School, Birmingham, and King William College, Isle of Man.

When assembling the chart above I was struck by the fact that although it did tell us which in truth are 'the great rugby schools,' in regard to keeping England well supplied with players, I was disappointed when I came to listing the great players they had turned out. I had expected that most of the big names of English rugby would be there. Far from it. With some schools such as Uppingham, Sherborne and Harrow, although featuring on the list, I was at a loss to find any player of note that they had produced. Where, I wondered, were Wakefield, Dickie Jeeps, Jeff Butterfield, Pullin, Peter Jackson, Richard Sharp etc.?

So I decided to look at it another way. I went through the list of England's leading cap winners (apart from those mentioned above) and checked which schools they had been to. With this result:

Player		
W. W. Wakefield	Sedbergh	1920s
Tommy Voyce	?	1920s
C. A. Kershaw	RN Colleges	1920s
W. J. A. Davies	RN Colleges	1910–20s
J. S. Tucker	St Nicholas & St Leonard's Church School	1920s
Peter Cranmer	St Edward's School, Oxford	1920s
B. C. Gadney	Stowe	1930s
Don White	Wellingborough G. S.	1940–50s
'Nim' Hall	Worksop	1940–50s
Ted Woodward	Royal Grammar School,	1950s
	High Wycombe	1950s
Peter Jackson	King Edward VI High School, Birmingham	
Eric Evans	?	1950s
J. D. Currie	Bristol G. S.	1950s
M. S. Phillips	Arnold School, Blackpool	1950s
J. MacG. Kendall-Carpenter	Truro School	1950s
C. R. Jacobs	Oakham	1950–60s
Don Rutherford	Tynemouth H. S.	1960s
Richard Sharp	Blundells	1960s
John Finlan	Saltley G. S.	1960s
Colin McFadyean	Bristol G. S.	1960s
Phil Judd	Broad Street School, Coventry	1960s
Dickie Jeeps	Bedford Modern	1960s

Player		
Peter Robbins	Bishop Vesey's G. S.	1960s
Peter Larter	Churston Ferrers G. S.	1960–70s
Bob Hiller	Bec School	1960–70s
John Pullin	Thornbury G. S.	1960–70s
Chris Ralston	King William College I. O. M.	1970s
'Stack' Stevens	Leedstown H. S.	1970s
David Duckham	King Henry VIII G. S., Coventry	1970s
Fran Cotton	Newton-le-Willows G.S.	1970s
Peter Dixon	St Bees School	1970s

This would seem pointedly to bear out the fact that rugby, having started as and in England always having been regarded as the great Public Schools game, is now dominated by others than those of Public School background.

8. The Varsity Match

It is a great pity that a fixture such as the Varsity Match with its wonderful history going back more than 100 years should so sadly dwindle in significance and in public interest. It has not yet sunk to the depths in which Oxford and Cambridge cricket finds itself, but there is the constant worry that it may.

Just one year short of being as old as the Rugby Union itself, the annual encounter got under way when Oxford invited Cambridge to the Parks on February 10, 1872. Oxford wore dark blue and Cambridge a rather ducky shade of pink. Next season it was at Cambridge. But from then on it was felt that neither team should have the advantage of playing at home and there followed various neutral venues – the Oval, Blackheath and the Queen's Club ('Ah, the good old Queen's Club,' aged Oxbridge Buffs still say today) and since 1921 at Twickenham.

From the outset the fixture was a nursery for Internationals, not only English but for all the Home Counties and for the British Isles touring teams. So packed with University men were the early Lions sides that Cambridge still cling to the record of contributing more to them than any other single club.

Right through the pre-Great War period and between the wars, the Varsity Match was regarded as an extra Trial. Participating Blues were excused from playing in Possibles v. Probables matches, not only to avoid the risk of injury putting them out of the inter-University clash but also the Big Day on the first Tuesday of December was a very important shop window for the England selectors and for those of the other British national teams. Anything up to half of the 30 taking part in the Varsity Match could find themselves chosen for service with England, Ireland, Scotland or Wales.

A perfect example was in the 1924–25 season when the entire superb Oxford three-quarter line – Wallace-Aitken-Macpherson-Smith – was transplanted to the Scotland side, to become regarded as one of the greatest ever set of threes in International rugby. The 1924 All Blacks, having had what they labelled as the toughest match of their tour against Oxford, were the first to admit that the Scotland fixture being cancelled through an off-the-field controversy was the luckiest thing that could have happened to them. Meeting that quartet again, supported by the cream of Scottish players, they felt would surely have meant the end of their invincible record.

From across the years one can reel off such a list of Oxbridge stars on the International field that it would fill pages. Just as a sampling: Stoop, Poulton-Palmer, Wakefield, Aarvold, Cranmer, Marques, Currie, Sharp etc. (England), Viv Jenkins, Wilf Wooller etc. (Wales), Andy Mulligan etc. (Ireland), Bedell-Sivright, Munro, Drysdale, Gordon Waddell, Ken Scotland, Stewart Wilson etc. (Scotland).

But predominantly any list of Great Oxford and Cambridge Internationals is pre-war and immediately post-war, for it was in the 1960s that things ground to a virtual halt. I remember being with the young members of one of the big touring teams from overseas in the late 1960s when they were invited to watch the University game and the standard of rugby was so abysmal that they could only look at one another and say: 'Is this really the Varsity Match we've been brought up to believe is so great?'

Any national selectors who had been there would surely have been wasting their time. By the close of the 1960s the tradition of Oxford and Cambridge Blues being concurrently stars of the Varsity Match and of the International scene was well and truly at an end. Sharp for England and

Mike Gibson for Ireland were among the last of that illustrious breed.

And worse was to follow. As the mid-way point of the 1970s decade was coming up, not only was moving straight from the Varsity match into International rugby a thing of the past. Surveying the teams of the four Home Counties, who could be found who had any sort of contact with Oxbridge? Gibson was still around, even if showing signs of retirement. Gerald Davies of Wales had been to Cambridge on a post-graduate course. Peter Dixon got his first cap for England in a Championship match two years after he had left Oxford. Any others you can think of?

What is the explanation for this sorry decline of a once great fixture? There are two basic reasons.

In the first place, the powers-that-be at Oxford and Cambridge decided to put more accent on the academic side of acceptance of students. Never let it be said that Oxbridge in former times descended to the level of American universities, so keen to show up well in sports that the entrance exam for athletic types was said to consist of: 'Do you know who is President of the United States? Answer yes or no.' But at Oxford and Cambridge in the old days they *were* interested in students who had inclinations towards something beyond mere book learning – getting out on the rugby or cricket field, the running track, skiing, rowing and the other pastimes honoured by a Blue.

Cecil Rhodes, when he established his splendid scholarships for Dominion and other students, was fully aware of the fact that a university education was a fine thing but narrow, if it consisted merely of getting one's head into the books. He stipulated that no one could become a Rhodes Scholar unless, as well as his academic qualifications, he had facility at some sport.

Rhodes was right. How can a university be said to produce a really rounded-out person when he knows only what Chaucer wrote, what Kant decanted, what Newton promulgated?

Today's bosses at Oxford and Cambridge, perhaps uneasy about the mushrooming red brick universities horning in on their virtual monopoly of turning out college graduates, have decided to keep their seats of learning academically ahead of the Non-U universities and in doing so are phasing out sports stars.

And the other major contributing factor in the decline of Oxbridge rugby . . .

As discussed in the chapter on the Public Schools, English rugby has now entered an era in which, if not yet the sport of the common man (as in South Africa, New Zealand and Wales), it at least has a much wider appeal. It is no longer 'rugger', with everything the term connotes . . . a jolly run-around by primarily Public School and Varsity types whose idea of training used not to amount to much more than giving up smoking on the morning of a match. Now the young players, drawn from all sorts of backgrounds, are fit, train conscientiously, are thoroughly coached, well drilled in the basic skills. It is a different image altogether from the old Varsity scene.

It is a shame that it is all changed now, for even in the recent past the Varsity Match brought us a great deal of rugby enjoyment and excitement. To choose but two examples that linger in the memory. From a Cambridge point of view, the wonderful performances of Mike Gibson, slicing his way through the opposition. From an Oxford vantage point, the superb half-back combination of Olwyn Brace and Mike Smith in the famous 1955 clash which automatically brought them International caps . . . such a pity that their respective parents had not been wise enough to bestow upon them qualifications for the same country, which would have avoided their being split to Wales and England and never reaching the same heights alone as they did together on that Tuesday in December when they dramatically reversed what was shaping up to be a certain Cambridge victory.

9. England Against the Visitors

We all know what a delightful diversity of touring teams we have visiting Britain now, from Fiji . . . Japan . . . Argentina . . . Tonga! But for generations before that it was merely those three regulars – the mighty All Blacks and Springboks and the not so formidable Wallabies (otherwise known as the Waratahs when they couldn't get any Queenslanders to join the New South Welshmen).

England, having invented the game and exported it to the colonies south of the equator, were soon to find that it was the pupils teaching the master in no uncertain terms. From the time of the first tour here by a national side – New Zealand in 1905 – thirty years were to elapse before England could manage to win an International against any country which came on tour.

Tours of Britain by overseas teams had in fact started in the 1888–89 season, with a privately organised visit by a side always misnamed 'The Maoris' in British record books and correctly designated the New Zealand Native Team in their home land. The tour was promoted by the team's captain, Joe Warbrick, an All Black who was later to have the odd distinction of being the only International rugby player ever killed in a volcanic eruption. His side, which was made up of *pakehas* (whites) as well as Maoris, he called the New Zealand Native Team to indicate that it was drawn purely from players born and bred in his country, the word 'native' being given the wrong connotation when they arrived here.

England beat that barn-storming side (they played 74

matches on their world-girdling tour) but official touring of this country did not start until Dave Gallaher's 1905 All Blacks, whose progress through England was, to put it mildly, devastating. Their record: played 27, won 27, points for 704, against 15. Only four of those 27 teams managed even a single score against the visitors!

In the post mortem that followed it was felt that a basic reason for the disaster was that those who had drawn up the itinerary had erred badly. The majority of fixtures had been against mere clubs. How could one expect the club players of Hartlepool, for instance, to do any better against a national touring team than be beaten 63–0?

So for the next tour by Paul Roos's Springboks in 1906–7, the English fixtures were all raised to county level or above. It would be nice to be able to say that this meant that it was a different kettle of fish altogether. Unfortunately it wasn't. The Springboks rode almost as roughshod over England's stiffer opposition. Played 19, won 18, one drawn, points for 399, against 30. There was solace, however, in the fact that the defeats had not been so heavy and England in the International did manage to hold the tourists to a draw.

As will be seen in the statistics of tours to England given in the back of the book, the Home Country was to have more success against Australian touring teams, which started coming here in 1908, but as the regular tours by New Zealand and South Africa unfolded it became apparent that these two countries could tour England and only as if by accident lose a match. London Counties achieved a lone victory against the 1912 Springboks. The 1924 All Blacks beat every English side they met. Midland Counties managed a single victory, but a notable one, against the 1931–32 South African tourists.

Notable because perhaps still to be rated as the greatest victory by an English regional team over one of the major touring sides was that win by Leicester Midlands against Bennie Osler's 1931–2 Springboks. It was not so much that they won. It was the manner of their doing it.

That particular South African touring party, unbeaten anywhere else, was such a formidable side. Names to conjure with like Brand, Zimmerman, Osler, Craven, Mostert, Nel and Bergh. Names to juggle with like J. F. van Niekerk, A. J. van der Merwe and J. H. van der Westhuizen. Included in the massive pack were M. M. (Boy) Louw and S. C. Louw, in those days when all the brothers and cousins made Louw the great family name of South African rugby.

And in beating that fearsome opposition Leicester Midlands did not merely scrape home. They outclassed them and in the course of it piled up the highest number of points ever recorded against a major touring side here or abroad – not excluding the 23 the Barbarians inflicted on the All Blacks at Cardiff in 1973.

They called it 'Slow's Match' because a young, inexperienced fly-half named Charlie Slow chose that day on which to give a performance he was never again to come anywhere near for his club, Northampton, or in his single appearance for England in 1934. To say he was sensational would be putting it mildly. The game had barely started before he had a dropped goal to the Midlanders' credit. Then he went over for two tries. He then went on to make two more of his team's next three tries and by the time it was all over had supporters fighting for the privilege of buying him drinks in the hectic celebrations in Leicester on the night of that famous victory.

But in all fairness, although it was young Charlie Slow who put the whipped cream on the top, the man really responsible was big (6 ft. 1 in., 16 st. 3 lb.) Ireland forward George Beamish, just recently returned with the Lions from New Zealand, where he had been acclaimed as the best forward the British Isles had ever sent out there. Beamish led the Midland forwards who subdued the Springbok pack, without which no victory was ever in sight against the South Africans. And how often was it done in that era in which the huge, rock-hard Afrikaners used to bulldoze their way upfield with Bennie Osler stitching the touchline from behind them? Beamish by example inspired his fellow forwards to lay the foundation for Slow and their other backs to exploit.

Leading 4–0 from the outset, 14–3 after twenty minutes, 19–6 at half-time . . . that was the pattern throughout the match, the Midlands constantly going ahead and the Springboks never able to catch them, no matter how hard they tried. Six times the South Africans scored, including no fewer than four tries by that great burly wing Morrie Zimmerman, but always they were in arrears, to finish soundly beaten by 30 points to 21.

In 1935–36 the All Blacks looked like carrying on the amazing record of New Zealand of beating every English side they met, only to stumble at the last hurdle. In 1905, in 1924–25 and up to the last match of the 1935–36 tour the All Blacks had beaten 61 English teams on the trot.

Then came an historic Saturday afternoon at Twickenham – January 4, 1936. The overall story of the All Blacks' tour up until then was that although having disposed of everything in the English provinces, Ulster had given them trouble to the extent of a 3–3 draw, Swansea had beaten them 11–3 and they had just come up from the Principality very unhappy about Wales beating them 13–12 in the last minute thanks, *they* felt to a lucky bounce coupled with a hint of obstruction. They wanted dearly to complete the tour with a sound victory over England which would scrub that from their minds.

Prince Alexander ('Obo') Obolensky, late of St Petersburg, currently at Oxford, was to prove that he had other ideas about that.

For anyone who saw the second of his two tries which were the key factors in the frustration of the All Blacks it is still vivid in the memory as one of the greatest International tries ever scored.

Playing on the right wing, the tall, blond, long-striding Russian had already scored a fine try in his legitimate corner of the goal area and this had quite a bearing on what he got up to for his second.

He was positioned near the right-hand touchline in his own half at the end of the backline when a scrum went down just inside the All Black half on England's left. The route from the scrum to Obolensky was, conventionally, Gadney-Candler-Cranmer-Gerrard (all good true-blue English names) until reaching The Flying Slav. But when it got as far as Cranmer in midfield he made a half break and after ten or fifteen yards transferred inside to supporting fly-half Candler.

Exercising rugby know-how not common among Russians, Obolensky deserted his post on the right wing, running in-field to take a pass from Candler. This created more than a little confusion among the All Blacks. In those days, when English back play was largely built around the idea of shipping the ball out along the line as quickly as possible to get the wing into action with a minimum of delay, all the defence was heading over towards Obolensky's wing to make sure this time of blocking the man who had outpaced them previously to his corner flag. Obolensky, ball in hand, decided in a flash to move across this defensive tide. He headed for the other corner flag.

Committed to going to their left the New Zealand backs and any of their forwards who had managed to be up with the play, all had to change direction. And through the scattered, wrong-footed defenders went Obolensky, to round full-back Gilbert and touch down where left-wings normally do their scoring.

Demoralisation naturally set in among the All Blacks after that and England were to finish up with a crushing 13–0 victory, invariably attributed by New Zealand rugby historians to All Black staleness after a long, tough tour, although of course there is nothing more calculated to make a team look stale than an opponent deciding that the day has come for him to play a blinder.

However, this was an isolated triumph for England's national side against the major touring teams in the pre-war era. After the war when touring was resumed it was the same sad story through the 1950s and 1960s of all English teams being beaten by the New Zealand and South African tourists, save for a solitary win by London Counties over the 1951–2 Springboks, which earned them a stuffed springbok head, to be seen in the Committee Rooms at Twickenham, screwed firmly to the wall to prevent souveniring.

Although it was different down in Wales, where clubs and the national side were always giving the tourists trouble, in England rugby followers had perforce to become philosophic about the visitors. Watching the touring sides in action took on a pattern. Supporters would go to the local ground to see the latest Blacks or Boks and in the opening stages would have high hopes of their lads making heroes of themselves and recording a triumph over the invaders. But gradually the tourists would assert themselves and then it was just a matter of sitting back and enjoying rugby played with expertise that the home team could never summon.

What else could one do when, during more than 60 years of tours, only one English team had ever beaten the All Blacks and only three had had isolated wins against the Springboks?

But then, as the 1960s were drawing to a close, came the revolution.

The turning point was the 1967 All Black tour. This was an improvised affair, hastily arranged when the New Zealand visit to South Africa that year had been cancelled. Those All Blacks slaughtered everything England put up against them – 'men against boys' was how it was described. And it was the best possible thing that could have happened to English rugby.

You see, the All Blacks had toured here in 1963–64 and normally there would have been a gap of some ten years before they came again. Instead, because of this impromptu tour, the English found themselves being massacred twice in the space of a mere three years. This stung them into action. Bowing to the All Blacks and the Springboks tour after tour must stop. The reason they always beat us was all too apparent. They have, and always have had, a highly developed system of coaching and training, in contrast to our casual, almost off-hand attitude towards preparation for a rugby match. If we were to avoid for ever being humbled we must do something about it, we must take a leaf out of their book. So – coaches were appointed, rigid training schedules introduced. And it was amazing how quickly the effects were to be seen.

When the Springboks came again in 1969–70, far from carrying all before them they were beaten by an English side (Oxford) in their very first match, numerous closely fought matches included their being lucky to emerge with a 3–3 draw against Western Counties and in the International England recorded her first ever victory against South Africa.

Then when the Seventh All Blacks came in 1972–73, the

third English team they met – North West Counties – struck from the rugby record books that statistic that had been there for 67 years: 'No English team other than the national side has ever beaten the All Blacks.' They scored their historic 16–14 win over the tourists at Workington. And not to be outdone, Midland Counties followed this up by beating them 16–8 at Moseley.

These indications that England had entered a new era in which they would no longer play permanent second fiddle to South Africa and New Zealand were then underlined in red ink when the Home country visited each of her former colonies and won each Test – something that had never been done before. But that is dealt with in the chapter about England on tour. Suffice to say here that gone for ever are the days when the English rugby fan bought his ticket for Home Side v the All Blacks or the Springboks knowing in his heart of hearts that it was just a matter of how many his team would be beaten by and how entertainingly or otherwise the beating would be inflicted.

10. *The Lions' Share*

Although the British rugby team had started touring in 1888 it was not until 1924 that they got the nickname of the Lions, when South African newspapers coined the term so handy for headlines from the insignia on the team tie. Officially the tourists were, and still are, the British Isles Rugby Union Team but before they became popularly known as the Lions it was not without some justification that on their tours to the then colonies of Australia, New Zealand and South Africa they were usually referred to locally as 'the English team'. From the outset each touring party was dominated by England players.

At time of writing there have been 19 Lions tours. It was not until the twelfth, to South Africa in 1950, that a team set out from Britain with more players from another of the Home Countries – Wales – rather than from England. At that point Britain had been represented at rugby overseas by 38 Scotsmen, 44 Irish, 52 Welsh . . . and 143 Englishmen.

It would be nice to be able to say that this reflected the fact that from the 1880s right through to the modern post-war era England was the dominant force in British rugby; they provided all the stars for the Lions tours; more English players were worthy of selection for Britain than all three of the other Home Countries combined.

But a rugby cynic in Cardiff, say, or Edinburgh or over in Ireland would be quick to point out that it is an interesting coincidence that the early Lions tours were all conducted by the English Rugby Union and also that the first British team not to be dominated by England players was for the first tour organised by the newly formed (in 1949) Four Home Rugby Unions Tours Committee, the permanent body which now handles all tours from and to Britain.

One must be fair and agree that England, being the senior Rugby Union, took the initiative in the pioneer days of overseas tours and not unnaturally they tended mainly to call on their own players. What is surprising, however, is that when they went atouring they invited any players at all from the three other Home Countries.

Why didn't England just tour alone?

New Zealand had set a precedent for them, being the first national side ever to undertake an overseas tour, to Australia in 1884. You may say that naturally New Zealand toured alone because of her isolated position on the map. But that wasn't necessarily so. When the Great War came in 1914 New Zealand was not considered of sufficient maturity to have her own army. She was lumped in with Australia as the Australian and New Zealand Army Corps – the Anzacs. Perhaps not at war but at rugby New Zealand by 1914 had well and truly established herself as a world power.

It is an interesting bit of conjecture to wonder what course world rugby would have taken if for the first overseas tour by a team from the British Isles the Rugby Football Union had elected to go it alone and tour purely and simply as England. Doubtless the other Home Countries would have followed this example of touring individually and one thing certain is that by the 1960s, when belatedly the four Home Unions *did* go on tour separately, they would have had touring expertise that would have produced much better results.

But would we have preferred England, Scotland, Ireland and Wales to have had separate tours from the outset? That way we would have been denied the pleasure and excitement that have been brought to us by that most popular of touring teams – the British Lions.

For the record, England players having dominated the Lions up until World War II, their representation in the post-war era has taken third place to Wales and Ireland in the eight tours 1950 to 1974:

Welsh	Irish	English	Scots
89	64	60	43

The overall picture for all 19 tours, however, reflects the head start England got when the Lions were cubs:

English	Welsh	Irish	Scots
203	140	107	81

That first tour, to Australia and New Zealand, in *1888* had been suggested to the Rugby Football Union by three England Test cricketers back from Australia with reports of enthusiasm there for rugby. One of the three, A. E. Stoddard, of Middlesex (cricket) and Blackheath (rugby), was to go on the tour as player-manager and took over as captain when R. L. Seddon was drowned while sculling on the Hunter River in New South Wales.

It is interesting to hear complaints from today's jet-set rugby tourists about the ardours of undertaking a major tour. The 22 players of the 1888 British side did a nine-month tour playing 54 matches (19 of them under Australian Rules), travelling by ship and leaky coastal packet boat, in embryonic trains and horse-drawn coaches on primitive country roads. Typical of the conditions in the colonies in those pioneer days was an item on the sports page of a New Zealand paper: 'Our footballers started yesterday for Kawakawa and if they ever get there, which is doubtful, they are going to play a match.' Are we getting soft?

No Tests were played by those 1888 pathfinders and of their 35 rugby matches they lost only two – against Auckland and Taranaki.

It is surprising that R. L. Aston, of Blackheath, won only two caps for England because he was far and away the hero of the next tour, in *1891* to South Africa. A three-quarter standing 6 ft. 3 in. and weighing 15 st., even in that land of big men he came to be regarded with awe. The locals could not understand how a man of those proportions could have such mobility and pace. 'When in possession in full flight for the line,' they wrote of him, 'he was almost impossible to bring to earth.' He scored 30 tries, an all-time record for a British tourist, in fact a record for a player on tour from any country second only to New Zealander Jimmy Hunter's 44 for the 1905 All Blacks in Europe.

Aston had much to do with that 1891 side returning home the most successful rugby team ever to have gone on tour. They played 19 matches and won them all and had it not been for a solitary try conceded in their first game would have put up the staggering performance of having whitewashed their opponents.

There is little to be said about England's contribution to the next tour, in *1896* again to South Africa. If ever the Irish took over a Lions tour and made it their own, on the field and off, this was it and one can read all about those roistering characters of the 1896 team in that admirable book, *The Men in Green.**

There is one other interesting aspect, however. We shall see shortly that the selection of British teams and of the teams for each of the Home Countries is very much divorced and this showed itself right from the early days. One wonders what was happening between the British and the England selectors whereby Aston, star of the previous tour, could rate only two Home Internationals. Now on this tour the Rev. M. Mullineux, also of Blackheath, performed sufficiently well at fly-half to be chosen as captain of the next Lions tour. Yet he was never capped for England.

It is interesting that in *1899* rugby in Australia was sufficiently strong to warrant their being hosts for a major tour all of their own. Shortly after this, however, Rugby League was introduced there and since that Non-U game seems to have been designed specially to appeal to the larrikin element in Australia it gained such a stranglehold that as we know that country is now only a side trip for Lions teams on their way to New Zealand.

As just mentioned, Blackheath's Rev. M. Mullineux was captain of this 1899 side but once more the English contingent was overshadowed – this time by Gwyn Nicholls, of Cardiff, the solitary Welshman in the team. He was the great crowd-puller of the tour, Australians tending to agree with the views of Welsh rugby historians past and present

* *Published by Pelham Books Ltd.*

which range from Nicholls being 'the finest centre Wales have ever produced' to 'the greatest rugby player of all time'.

There was a very good reason why on this tour England had no players worthy of mention in the same breath with Gwyn Nicholls and why in the following three tours – to South Africa in *1903* and to Australia and New Zealand in *1904* and *1908* – they similarly contributed to the Lions no players who could be regarded as star performers. It was a direct outcome of the damage done to English rugby by the Northern Union breakaway of 1893.

As we have pointed out earlier, England were International Champions in the 1891–2 season and 18 slim seasons were to elapse before they again came out on top. And in the five tours by the British Isles in that period – the 1896, 1899, 1903, 1904 and 1908 tours – it was players from Home Countries other than England who monopolised the limelight.

But by the time the *1910* tour of South Africa came along it was a different story. England had emerged from the doldrums with a vengeance. In the 1909–10 season at home they had roared back on to the International scene by winning the Championship with complete conviction, beating Wales, Scotland and France and being denied the Grand Slam merely through a draw with Ireland. And to the British party that set off for South Africa they contributed a young man just turned 20 who had been the key figure in their triumph in the Home Internationals and who was to dominate the tour as no other Lion has ever done before or since. (Correspondence from Barry John fans should be addressed to the author care of the publishers.)

Elsewhere in this book (Chapter 12) I go into full ecstatic detail about the achievements of C. H. ('Cherry') Pillman. Suffice to say here that one South African rugby writer said of him : 'He played a game apparently invented by himself.' His self-developed wing forward play set the model for South Africans to evolve the No. 8 expertise brought to its apex by such Springboks as Muller and Hopwood. He topped the individual points table with six tries and 21 kicks at goal. For the hell of it he played stand-off half in one of the three Tests and made it a great day for Britain by engineering the sensational winning try. Such was his impact on the South Africans that he was to be given the supreme accolade of that 1910 visit by the Britishers being referred to henceforth as 'Pillman's Tour'.

The most notable absentee from the *1924* side in South Africa was England's captain, W. W. Wakefield, the greatest forward and team leader of his time.

Unavailability has long been the bane of Britain on the tour, something which has never greatly worried New Zealand or South Africa, where the importance of rugby is such that ways and means are always found around loss of earnings or interruption of university studies, the two main reasons for a player announcing himself unable to devote the time for a long rugby tour.

Besides Wakefield, other England players of world class who have stayed at home when the Lions were on tour include: Stoop, Poulton-Palmer, Kershaw and Davies, Cranmer, Currie (the other half of the famous Marques and Currie duo), Eric Evans (at the time second most capped England player with 30 but never a Lions cap), Jacobs (29 England caps), Kendall-Carpenter and Judd. (Although not really the function of this book, we would add other great rugby names who were never Lions such as Ireland's Ernie Crawford, Scotland's Gracie and Wilson Shaw, Wales's Arthur Gould and Wooller, to mention but a few to stress how unavailability has weakened British sides.)

It was a great pity Wakefield could not tour in 1924 because it broke up the Wakefield-Voyce-Blakiston combination which had pioneered backrow play as we know it today and which had played such an important part in England's domination of the International Championship in the early 1920s. Voyce and Blakiston were on the tour, but without the architect of their fast breaking back-of-the-scrum techniques they were not nearly as effective.

Captained by Dr Ronald Cove-Smith, then England's most capped player after Wakefield, the team unfortunately returned home with the worst record of any Lions side before or since. Only nine of the 21 matches were won. The team was plagued by injuries. For some odd reason three full-backs had been sent, two of them English. It was just as well, for one of these two, W. S. Gaisford, was injured in the initial practice and took no part in the tour proper; the other, T. E. Holliday, broke his collarbone in the first match. Which placed quite an onus on Scotland's great but sorely overworked full-back, 'Darkie' Drysdale. Injuries became such a problem by mid-tour that H. J. Davies, of Newport, had to get the quickest ship out to South Africa to bolster the depleted back division and retired Irish International W. Cunningham, who happened to be living in Johannesburg, also was pressed into service.

As well as the difficulty of trying to carry on the tour with a high percentage of cripples (in those days before quick replacements by air), another contributing factor to their poor showing was that it just so happened that at that period South Africa was entering one of its golden eras. Even when fully fit it was asking something of a visiting team to outshine such new and established Springbok stars as Bennie Osler and Pierre Albertyn in the backs and Theuns Kruger, Phil Mostert and Frank Mellish up front.

With the *1930* team in Australia and New Zealand I can bring first-hand knowledge to bear on writing about the Lions. My father was Hon. Dental Surgeon to the Auckland Rugby Union, a sinecure that had come his way through the Secretary being a close friend, and by virtue of his office we got tickets to all the big matches. Thus it was that in the old wooden members stand at Eden Park (still retained for sentimental reasons), I saw my first Lions team in action.

Let us dispose initially of those non-English stars who impressed me and who still linger in the memory of New Zealanders. Policeman Jack Bassett, Welsh full-back, had none of the charisma of his opposite number in the Tests, George Nepia, even though then at the end of his career, but he was solid and safe and at all times reassuring for any team to have behind them as a last line of defence. George Beamish, the huge Leicester aggressor, was acclaimed as the greatest forward ever to have visited New Zealand. By rights, since he was based in the Midlands, he should have been a player for England to be for ever proud of but by an unfortunate accident of parentage Ireland were able to claim him. And Ivor Jones, of Llanelli, that superb loose forward who was such an everywhere man that on several occasions it was no trouble at all for him to play in the backs when the Lions were beset by injuries.

Sobey and Spong, of Old Millhillians, were expected to establish themselves on this tour as the new Kershaw and Davies. Unfortunately Sobey was injured out of the tour in the first match and they were unable to realise the potential they had shown as a half-back duo at school and with the Old Boys. The powerfully-built, elusive Roger Spong carried on at fly-half, to become one of the outstanding successes of the team despite the efforts of the New Zealand breakaways to do him grievous bodily harm and to establish a tradition carried on by Kyle, Cliff Morgan, Risman, Sharp and Barry John of the Lions invariably having a great crowd-pleaser in that position.

An Englishman captained the side – Doug Prentice, a forward who had not had a particularly distinguished International career (only three caps) but his name was to be in the public eye for many years. A replica of his signature was on all tickets for Twickenham from 1947 to 1962, when he was Secretary to the R.F.U. He did not shine especially on the field for the 1930 Lions, his role being more important off the field where he and Manager James Baxter had more than a little diplomatic work to do in regard to the very testy controversies that cropped up over variations in the rules that New Zealand had developed in the 22 years since a British team had last been there.

Shining on the field was in the capable hands of other Englishmen. Carl Aarvold, for instance. A classic three-quarter with a beautiful running action and graciously deceptive swerve. It was to no avail, however, on one well remembered occasion in the Third Test when, with Blackheath teammate Tony Novis outside him, and only Nepia to beat a certain try was on. With his well-known tactic of back-pedalling to confuse oncoming players as to when to pass, the wily Maori was able to nail him ball and all and as he got up afterwards Aarvold said: 'You bastard! Where did you learn that trick?' More dignified has been his language during his distinguished career as His Honour Judge Sir Carl Aarvold, Recorder of London.

In the *1938* tour to South Africa the English, with nine, were the strongest contingent but the Welsh were the dominant force. They had such stars as full-back Viv Jenkins, scrum-half Hadyn Tanner and the hooker South Africans regarded as the best ever to visit them, 'Bunny' Travers of Newport. Of the nine Englishmen four were never England players and the others only minor Internationals. One of the two England stars of that period who would have been very useful against the strong Craven-led opposition were Peter Cranmer, who was unable to travel, and brilliant full-back 'Tuppy' Owen-Smith, who was not available because after being a Rhodes Scholar at Oxford he had reverted to being a South African again and in the previous year had returned to his home country to set up in medical practice.

As far as life in general was concerned the 1950s were a dreary decade but oddly enough it saw a blossoming of British rugby. The first of the decade's three Lions tours – to Australia and New Zealand in *1950* – wasn't all that good, especially for England since it was her lowest ever representation with only three (Ivor Preece, Gordon Rimmer and Vic Roberts). It was very much a Welsh affair, with 14 of the Grand Slam Wales team in the side, and it was perhaps surprising that the best they could do was merely draw one of the four New Zealand Tests. However, the next two Lions teams of the '50s were among the best and most popular Britain has ever sent abroad.

Until the achievement of the 1971 Lions the *1955* side in South Africa was acknowledged as the best British team this century, coming closest (with a 2–2 tally) to that elusive winning of a Test series against the Springboks or the All Blacks. Their 23–22 victory in the first of the four matches against South Africa is regarded by leading rugby historians as the greatest Test ever.

Before a record rugby crowd of 100,000 in what sports writers like to call the cauldron of Jo'burg's Ellis Park ... Wales's great Cliff Morgan making all five of the Lions' tries and scoring one of them himself and establishing a great reputation with South Africans ... Ireland's Pedlow

England v. Australia at Highbury, 1924. *Below:* England on tour. A scene during the England v. New Zealand game at Lancaster Park, Christchurch, in June 1963. Don Clarke (No. 1) has just kicked a goal from a mark from 60 yards

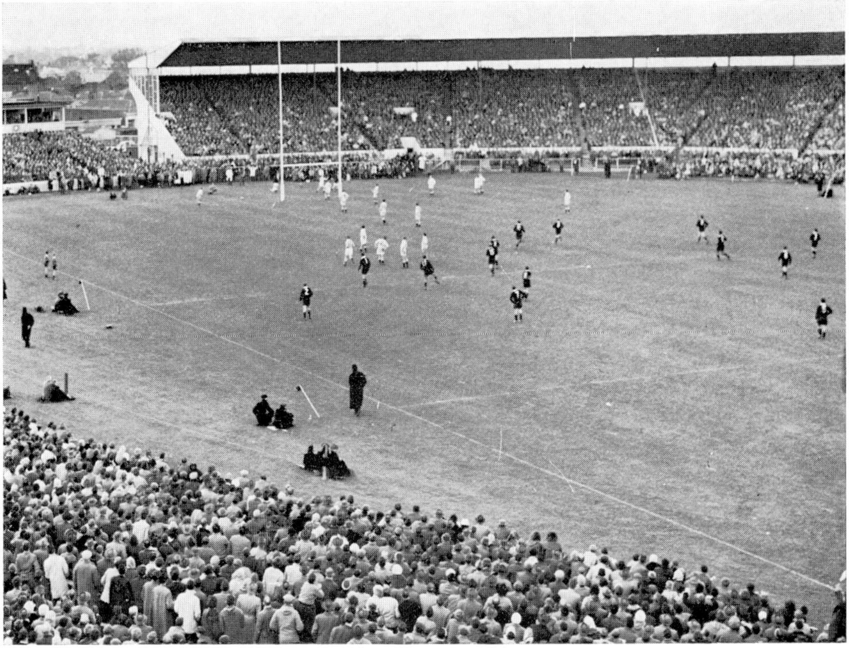

Bob Hiller, renowned for the accuracy and length of his kicking, won 18 caps for England in the late 1960s and early 1970s. Here he is pictured after Harlequins had won the Middlesex 7-a-side tournament in 1967. *Below left:* Peter Jackson, one of England's leading threequarters in the late 1950s and early 1960s, pictured here in a Lions' jersey during the game against Waikato on the 1959 Lions tour of New Zealand. *Below right:* Roger Uttley, a 1974 Lion and outstanding forward in English rugby in the 1970s

The famous occasion during the 1925 New Zealand tour of Great Britain when Cyril Brownlie was sent off in the match against England at Twickenham. *Below:* Training. England scrum-half Jan Webster looks on as the pack practise scrummaging in preparation for the game against Wales in March 1974

The demo tour. The 1969–70 Springbok tour is probably better remembered for events off the field than on it. This is a scene before the opening match of the tour, against Oxford University at Twickenham

Jan Webster gets the ball away to England's fly-half Martin Cooper during the special charity match against France at Twickenham on 20th April 1974

and Tony O'Reilly scurrying along the wings for their tries. A great side for running with the ball in this and all their matches and as vital to the scintillating back play as the spectacular Morgan and O'Reilly were the three Test regulars from England – Jeeps behind the scrum and Butterfield and Davies in the centre.

We mentioned a little earlier that selectors for the British Isles were quite divorced from those who picked the Home Country teams. Dickie Jeeps was a shining example of this. The great little Northampton scrum-half was uncapped when chosen for this 1955 tour and the fact that the men who chose the Lions knew what they were about was borne about by Jeeps taking his place as one of the greatest Lions ever, eventually setting up a record of three tours and 13 Test appearances.

The *1959* team in Australia and New Zealand was so star-studded that merely to start listing the team sounds like a rugby hall of fame: Scotland's Ken Scotland, Waddell, McLeod etc . . . Wales's Terry Davies, B. V. Meredith etc . . . Ireland's O'Reilly, Mulligan, Dawson (capt.), etc . . . Could England's representation stand up in such company? Certainly they could. Butterfield, Risman, Horrocks-Taylor, Marques . . . and the one who for New Zealanders was the greatest crowd-pleaser of them all – Peter Jackson.

With talent like that it wasn't surprising that, including a couple of matches in Canada on the way home, they were to pile up by far the greatest number of tries (165) and highest aggregate points (842) of any Lions side and they were prevented from being the most successful this century purely and simply because of the presence in the All Blacks of one Don Clarke, who all alone won the notorious first Test, 18–17, with his six penalties, and provided the winning points in the second and third. His efforts to make it a grand slam were fortunately frustrated in the final Test by Bev Risman's sensational match-winner when he switched to the blind side for a 35-yard try still talked about in New Zealand.

But not talked about as much as right-wing Jackson's overall performance on that 1959 tour. As Tony O'Reilly put it: 'Jackson was so popular with New Zealand crowds that the Lions were asked to provide him with a one-wheel cycle and three juggling balls so that he could keep spectators entertained while play was not on his side of the field.'

Compared to the splendours of the 1959 tour the *1962* visit to South Africa was a somewhat drab affair. It had not been expected that it would be. Quite the contrary, for the man designated as the star of the side had just burst forth upon a grateful English rugby public as one of the most exciting fly-halves for many a long day. Unfortunately, early in the tour Richard Sharp, who had justifiably been expected to be the inspiration of the team, was put out of action for six weeks with a facial injury.

Not for one moment would one suggest that the South Africans deliberately decided that it would be helpful to them in the Tests if a key man such as Sharp were put on the sidelines. But their sports writers did agree that when, in the match before the first Test, Mannie Roux hospitalised Sharp with a rather forceful tackle it was 'an unhappy accident'.

The outcome was that for a lengthy stretch of the tour that vital midfield position where so much of the strategy of a team originates was occupied by Gordon Waddell, of Scotland, or England's own Mike Weston. Both of these were noted, or more accurately one should say on occasions notorious, for their liking for tactical kicking, so that for much of the tour the exciting running and open back play which was the Sharp approach was as absent as it had been characteristic of the 1959 tourists.

After a great unbeaten start to their tour in eight matches in Australia, including a record 31–0 over Australia, the *1966* Lions went on to do badly in New Zealand, losing eight matches including all the Tests, and then succeeding in achieving an unusual defeat by a provincial team in Canada. Led without distinction by Mike Campbell-Lamerton, of Scotland, who must have been as surprised as anybody that he got the captaincy over the obvious choice, Wales's Alun Pask, the team was also not well managed or coached. Of talent there was plenty . . . Stewart Wilson at full-back, Hinshelwood and Stuart Watkins on the wings, Mike Gibson and Dai Watkins in midfield, great forwards such as hookers Kennedy and Laidlaw, McBride, Telfer, Lamont . . . but individually they could not triumph over the bad morale engendered by mismanagement. England's representation of five (Rutherford, Savage, McFadyean, Weston and Powell), the second lowest of any Lions tour, had little to blame for the overall poor showing.

As the 1960s were drawing to a close Bob Hiller had established himself as the great favourite of the English crowds but when he set off with the *1968* Lions for South Africa there seemed little likelihood that he would have much chance to shine. The reason was simple. Ireland's full-back Tom Kiernan was captain and naturally he would play in most of the matches including all the Tests. But Hiller contrived to make his mark, setting up a record for the quickest 'ton' in international tours – 104 points in the mere eight matches in which he played.

It was a team beset by injury (Barry John played in merely four matches, as just one example), yet they were able to get through their provincial programme with just one defeat, by Transvaal. But it was too much to expect the injury weakened side to pull off the Test series, lost by three and a draw.

England made little contribution to the backs, apart from Hiller, Keith Savage being the only other Englishman on hand but hooker Pullin and Horton, Larter, Coulman and Bryan West did valuable work up front.

The *1971* Lions in Australia and New Zealand – this was a great tour, the first time this century that the British Isles had won a Test series against their great rivals New Zealand or South Africa.

One might say that in an odd sort of way it was England's David Duckham who won the series for the Lions. In the final Test they were 2–1 up and needed only to draw to win the rubber. As the match was nearing its end left-winger Duckham found himself hemmed in when he got possession from a mêlée on his touchline and in what, in the event, turned out to be a flash of genius he flung the ball Middlesex-sevens style far infield for John Williams. The Welsh full-back, brilliant in so many aspects of rugby, did not number drop-kicking as one of his major talents. But on this occasion he let fly from 50 yards for the ball to sail between the posts and give the Lions the three extra points which assured them of a 14–14 draw.

It is of course over-simplification to say that Duckham was the hero of the tour, in view of all that had gone before. The tremendous success of the Lions – the first Test was the solitary match they lost in New Zealand – stemmed from a combination of various factors . . . the superb coaching of Carwyn James and captaincy of John Dawes . . . the great Edwards-John-Gibson midfield trio . . . Barry John's record 180 points . . . and the forwards who erected the platform for the success of the backs – men such as McLauchlan and McLoughlin, McBride, Quinnell, John Taylor and Delme Thomas.

And not the least among those men up front who denied the New Zealanders their traditional forward superiority were the Test regulars from England – John Pullin, hooking, and Peter Dixon in the loose.

In *1974* Mr Harold Wilson, the then but I hope not now Prime Minister, annoyed a great number of people, not only rugby followers, when he announced that the British Embassy in South Africa would not give a welcoming party to the Lions and their Embassy staffs would shun their fellow-countrymen during their sojourn in the Republic. The reason was that the Labour Government did not approve of apartheid and of British rugby players competing against teams which were not chosen on a multi-racial basis.

The amusing thing is that although Mr Wilson was making a political gesture against the Lions by denying them British Embassy receptions in South Africa he was in fact doing them a great service. He relieved them of one of the most boring aspects of rugby tours. The functions come thick and fast on tour. The players don't mind having a get-together with men of their own age group where beer can be consumed and rugby chat exchanged, and they are not averse to chicks being present, to fill out the evening after the serious business of drinking and talking rugby is at an end. But what bores them stiff are official functions, with interminable speeches and older men buttonholing them to bang their ears with monologues about *their* great moments of glory and talk of players and events long in the past. Mr Wilson got an unspoken vote of thanks from the Lions for striking from their social list the Embassy functions at which it cannot only be the older men who are tedious. I remember an aside made to me by a suffering player at such a function: 'No shirt too young to stuff.'

But to deal with the more serious aspect of Mr Wilson's behaviour... He was no doubt sincere. He of course had every right to disapprove of a foreign country's internal policies and to make whatever gesture against that country which was within his power to make. But where one could take issue with him was on the score of his being inconsistent, to the point of being downright two-faced. South Africa is Britain's third biggest trading partner, with an exchange of trade amounting to not far short of £1,000,000 *per day.* One can be sure that the directors on the governing boards of the big South African companies with which Britain trades are not chosen on a multi-racial basis. South African trade delegations are most certainly not picked on a multi-racial basis. Why is it all right to have dealings with those teams and yet quite wrong to have dealings with South African rugby teams?

In spite of – and perhaps in some degree because of – the Labour Government's disapproval of the tour taking place, Willie John McBride's men proceeded to turn in the greatest performance ever put up by a British rugby side this century and with their unbeaten (21 wins, one draw) record to strike a blow for British sporting prestige on a par with Bannister's sub-4-minute mile, England's World Cup and Jacklin's British and US Open Victories.

The 1974 Lions were dominated by England and Wales with nine representatives each, followed by Ireland with eight and Scotland, six. But apart from the tremendous importance of McBride's super leadership, it was the Welsh who were the stars. Dr John Williams confirmed that he is the world's greatest full-back, and Gareth Edwards that he is the world's greatest scrum-half. Bennett added brilliant running with the ball to his known capabilities at kicking it tactically and between the uprights, until hampered late in the tour with a suspect leg. J. J. Williams on the wing did sensational things for a new boy in big time rugby. Windsor as hooker and Mervyn Davies as No. 8 were constantly praised by the South Africans, who are acknowledged experts in those two departments.

The English contingent was Evans, Old and Morley (replacement) in the backs, and the forwards Cotton, Burton, Ralston, Uttley, Neary and Ripley.

Evans had a tour which could be described as merely adequate and Morley could make little impact in merely two appearances. Likewise Alan Old had no real chance to show himself. He was unfortunately late-tackled out of the tour in his fourth match. A great pity because there was no question that as fly-half and place-kicker he would have taken over in the last two Tests from the not fully fit Phil Bennett.

Andy Ripley was a disappointment to his fans at home, not developing into the Lions star that had been expected. He was picked for merely nine of the 22 matches, was never really in contention for a Test place. Roger Uttley on the other hand became, to the surprise of everybody at home, a loose forward rather than his customary lock position; played in all the Tests, shared with Gareth Edwards the most appearances (16) on tour. One of the great successes, along with Fran Cotton, another of the tourists' most used players – 14 appearances, including all four Tests. With 'Mighty Mouse' McLaughlan and hooker Windsor, Cotton formed a front row of which it was said that they 'became a legend everywhere they went in South Africa.' Burton, Neary and Ralston, the other three of England's six forwards on tour, were serviceable members of the party, lock Ralston getting a cap in the final Test.

England could be said to have made an important contribution to the success of the tour through Test regulars Cotton and Uttley, but on this tour perhaps more than any other it was the general team effort that was the most telling factor. It was perhaps McBride's greatest asset as captain that he made them all feel that they were doing their share, even the mid-week 'reserves'. And symbolic of this important aspect of touring team morale was his assembling of his victorious side in the series-winning third Test as they came off the field to signal acknowledgement to the non-players in the stand.

11. England on Tour

From the time they invented rugby 140 years elapsed, during which they played host to many an overseas touring team, before England themselves ventured abroad.

When they embarked on this first, short (6-match) tour to New Zealand and Australia in 1963, they were the Five-Nations Champions. But unfortunately five of the key men who had helped them to the championship of Europe were not available – full-back Wilcox, wings Jackson and Roberts, fly-half Sharp and scrum-half Jeeps. It is a bit much to ask of a team to reproduce its best form when you rip out all their first-string backs except the two centres.

That reliable utility back Mike Weston, who captained the side, and centre Malcolm Phillips were there from the original team. A new boy, Hosen, filled in at full-back. Horrocks-Taylor with S. J. S. Clarke and Wintle did service for the Sharp-Jeeps combination. The forwards were at full strength, spearheaded by Godwin, Jacobs, Judd and Budge Rogers.

Everything started all right, with a good win against Wellington, but from then on it was all downbeat, not another match being won. The two Tests against New Zealand could, however, have been a different story, had it not been for the greatest match-winner of all time – Don Clarke – deciding to do a repeat performance of his single-handed humbling of the Lions in New Zealand four years before.

Still vididly remembered (and still rankling!) were his six penalties to beat the 1959 Lions in the first Test and his last-minute try which snatched the second away from them. Now against the 1963 English tourists his 15 points were the match-winning factor in New Zealand's 21–11 victory in the first Test and in the other . . . The scores were level at 6–6 with just a couple of minutes to go. Clarke fielded the ball inside his own half and claimed a mark. He signalled that rarity – a shot at goal from a mark, even more rare when you're in your own half! It wasn't on, of course, not even for the great Don Clarke, since in addition to the distance, the men on the mark could charge. But besides being the master with the boot, he was also no slouch when it came to gamesmanship. He started what appeared to be his run-up and the chargers charged. Clarke stopped in his tracks and appealed to the referee. He wasn't 'making to kick', he was merely going forward to change the position of the ball. No charge, a free kick, ordered the referee. And although the 60-yard boomer was admittedly a magnificent match-winner, it was just a little bit sullied.

ENGLAND IN NEW ZEALAND AND AUSTRALIA – 1963

Beat Wellington	14–9
Lost to Otago	9–14
Lost to NEW ZEALAND (First Test)	11–21
Lost to Hawke's Bay	5–20
Lost to to NEW ZEALAND (Second Test)	6–9
Lost to AUSTRALIA	9–18

Played 6, Won 1, Lost 5, Points: For 54, Against 91

Almost a decade was to pass before England were on tour again or in the immortal words of J. B. G. Thomas, on trek in South Africa.

The 1972 team was captained by John Pullin and all the current England stars apart from Duckham were available to travel. Doble at full-back, Old and Webster the half-backs . . . the great 'perm three from four' front row of Stack Stevens, Pullin, Burton and Cotton . . . Ralston and Larter in the boiler room . . . Ripley, Watkins and Neary on the loose.

But 'stars' was hardly the right word to use as they emplaned for South Africa, since unlike the 1963 tourists they did not go on tour fresh from triumphs at home. Exactly the opposite. They were holders of the Wooden Spoon, with not a point to their credit in the Five-Nations Championship. On form, no bookie would have given them a chance but just as the Form Guide can be meaningless in regard to picking winners at the races, this 1972 touring party upset all predictions.

In their 7-match tour they sailed through all the early opposition, only faltering slightly with a 13–13 draw against that toughest of provincial sides, Northern Transvaal, to come up to the final match – the Test at Jo'burg – unbeaten.

However, there had been a tendency in recent years for touring sides to dispose of South African provincial teams without too much difficulty, only to be humiliated by the full might of the Springboks. It had happened to the All Blacks in South Africa in 1970 – after slaughtering everything in the provinces, disaster in the Tests. So . . . England really couldn't be expected to round things off by winning the Big One.

It was a great match, of the see-sawing type in the early stages when England had twice to cancel out arrears and then, just on half-time, getting their noses ahead at 9–6 and never relinquishing their lead to wind up 18–9 victors.

In this historic win over South Africa in their first match with them on their own soil England's hero as far as points-scoring was concerned was Sam Doble, who seemed to be determined to prove that he could be just as prolific in international rugby as he had been season-after-season for Moseley. He piled up 14 of the 18 points with four penalties and the conversion of a try by winger Morley. But it was the team effort that had done it – the forwards holding and eventually getting mastery over the bigger Springbok pack, Jan Webster doing a great job at the base of the scrum, the backs stonewall tackling their opponents out of any chance to cross their line. And all under the inspired leadership of new England captain John Pullin.

ENGLAND IN SOUTH AFRICA – 1972

Beat Natal	19–0
Beat Western Province	9–6
Beat South African Federation XV	11–6
Beat South African (Bantu) XV	36–3
Drew with Northern Transvaal	13–13
Beat Griqualand West	60–21
Beat SOUTH AFRICA	18–9

Played 7, Won 6, Drew 1, Points: For 166, Against 58

There was only one home season between England's first, triumphant tour to South Africa and her next, the 1973 trip to Fiji and New Zealand. And quite a season it was. Everyone has always been expecting that by the law of averages some day all the countries in the Five-nations Championship would wind up the tournament with equal points. Which was precisely what happened in 1972–73. So by the time the new tour to the Antipodes came up, England were joint champions in Europe – with the four others.

The side chosen to go on tour had virtually the same pack as had done such good service in South Africa but there were some radical changes in the backs. Doble had fallen from favour and Rossborough and Jorden went in his place. Duckham was this time available for one of the wings and Squires on the other, and newcomer G. W. Evans had proved a good partner for Preece in the centre in the Home Internationals.

Coach John Elders had got them into good shape, but not for this tour. The original plan had been a visit to Argentina but terrorists had wrecked that with announced plans to molest the players. The Fiji-New Zealand 5-match tour was hastily arranged as a substitute.

The first game, against the popular Fijians in Suva, was almost a disaster. Jet-lag and the torrid heat in which they were asked to play were an excuse but nevertheless they were lucky to scrape home 13–12.

The rain and mud for their first match in New Zealand, against Taranaki, were no excuse, being far more familiar to them. They went down to the men in amber and black.

Wellington disposed of them, and then Canterbury, thanks mainly to Fergie McCormick kicking the important goals while the tourists' Rossborough and Old missed all of their shared nine attempts.

So, when they went to delightful Waitangi in the far north to prepare for the Test in Auckland they had the sad record of 'Played 3, Lost 3'. None of the locals gave them a chance. Still smarting from the Lions' first ever win in a series in New Zealand in 1971 and the unhappy 'Murdoch tour' of Europe in 1972–73, domestic feeling was that some amends could be made by the All Blacks thrashing these Poms.

As England's home supporters were to see for themselves, thanks to the miracle of New Zealand black-and-white television brought to them by satellite, it didn't happen that way.

Before a 55,000 crowd at Eden Park scrum-half Jan Webster seemed to be the hero. New Zealand were without Joe Karam, the little Lebanese-kiwi full-back who had been one of the few to come through with honours here in 1972–73; he was on some sort of vacation outside the country. As his stand-in the New Zealand selectors came up with a fellow named Lendrum, which was one of the best things that had happened to English rugby in many a year. Even allowing for the fact that there can be distortion on the TV screen, he appeared to be in all ways a first-class dud. It was from two of his mistakes – a bad clearance and a shocking stumble-fumble of a kick ahead – which allowed the ebullient Webster to latch on to the ball to set up two vital tries. This, coupled with his completely outshining Sid Going around the scrum, added up to a match-winning performance.

However, to single Webster out is a bit unfair to the other England players who took part in this first defeat ever inflicted on New Zealand on their own soil by any of the Home Countries. It had all been worked out by coach Elders and captain Pullin that the All Blacks could be beaten at their own formula of 'Sid Going and the back row'. With England's front five – Stevens-Pullin-Cotton, Ralston-Uttley – rising to the challenge of thoroughly outscrummaging the opposition, the platform was set up for Webster – linked with the Watkins-Ripley-Neary back row – to render Ian Kirkpatrick and his side-kicks ineffectual and to harass Going into a really bad match.

'An even better win than the one over the Springboks at Jo'burg,' said Pullin, proved now a great touring captain for England and obviously destined to wind up his outstanding career in overseas touring as first-string hooker, if not captain, of the Lions in South Africa in 1974. It was one of the big surprises of rugby that he was passed over by the British selectors.

ENGLAND IN FIJI AND NEW ZEALAND – 1973

Beat Fiji	13–12
Lost to Taranaki	3–6
Lost to Wellington	16–25
Lost to Canterbury	12–19
Beat NEW ZEALAND	16–10

Played 5, Won 2, Lost 3 Points: For 60, Against 70

12. The Greats of English Rugby

Down through the English rugby years, these men have stood out above their contemporaries:

1910s

Adrian Stoop

In assessing the stature of Stoop, one of the most important players in the history of the game, one must bear in mind two things. First, the stage of development rugby had reached when he came on the scene, and secondly, the state in which English rugby in particular was at the time.

In the first regard, when it is said that he revolutionised back play it does not mean (so I've found out!) that he merely brought a new dimension to the already established set-up. He did more than that. He established the set-up!

Born in 1883, when he started playing at Rugby School it was before the turn of the century and rugby was still primarily a mauling game. In his first year at the school the main law as to scrummaging read: 'A scrummage, which can only take place in the field of play, is when the ball is put down between players who have closed round on their respective sides and they shall endeavour to push their opponents back, and by kicking the ball, to drive it in the direction of the opposite goal line.' Heeling the ball? This was regarded as unethical, if not downright illegal. Apart from anything else, if you hooked the ball back didn't that automatically put your forwards offside? And during his progress through Oxford to the Harlequins early this century this attitude towards heeling persisted.

So one can see that Stoop's early days in rugby were not played in the sort of relationship forwards and backs have today. And the backs were not settled into the fixed positions we know now. Even in 1905 England in their match against the touring All Blacks at Crystal Palace played five three-quarters. Stoop came to the game when the two half-backs alternated as scrum-half depending on which side of the field play was, in the manner of centres switching. It was Stoop who saw the wisdom of having specialists behind the pack, i.e. a scrum- and a fly-half, the latter being the position he made his own, to set the pattern for future generations to follow.

By 1910 he had things organised and that date is an interesting one in that it was the focal point of the other reason why Stoop stands so high on the list of the Greats of England. It was he who spearheaded his country's revival after 18 years in the wilderness as far as the International Championship was concerned.

Having won it in 1892, England suffered the crippling setback of the breakaway of the Northern Union in the following year. As season followed season she was so weakened that it seemed she would never again get back to the same International level as the other Home Countries. Her first match for the opening of the 1910 International season on January 15 was chosen as the inaugural International for the newly completed Twickenham – against Wales. With the best will in the world nobody could hope for anything but further humility. The Welsh champions were fresh from two Grand Slam seasons, at the peak of their Golden Era.

Wales kicked off and Stoop fielded. In the tradition of the game in that period he should have kicked to touch. Instead he set off infield, invited the entire Welsh side to believe that that was the direction in which he was going to continue and then switched back towards the wing. The ball passed through various players, to reach centre Birkett, who put the burly F. I. Chapman over for Twickenham's first International try before the opposition had laid a hand on the ball.

This brilliant opening gambit by Stoop was something from which the Welsh were never able fully to recover and England recorded a famous victory, 11–6, which was to mean that they and not as expected Wales were to wind up champions that year. And thus it was that Stoop, in most dramatic fashion, signalled England's emergence from the doldrums. It was the end of Wales's Golden Era and the beginning of England's.

R. W. (Ronnie) Poulton-Palmer

Born in 1889 and educated at Rugby, Poulton-Palmer in his sadly short career, became one of the most admired England rugby players on and off the field.

The great England fly-half W. J. A. Davies played beside the majestic, fair-haired centre who had the uncanny knack of changing the length of his stride to deceive would-be tacklers in eight of his 17 Internationals and wrote of him: 'His easy grace and charm of manner, his versatility on the football field, that characteristic run of his are vivid impressions of probably the greatest figure that ever played rugby football.'

At Oxford before joining Harlequins, Poulton-Palmer scored five tries in his first Varsity Match, something never achieved before or since, to spearhead the biggest win (35–3) ever recorded by either side. His total of 24 points in his three appearances against Cambridge also is an all-time record for this fixture with more than 100 years of history behind it.

Welshman W. J. Townsend Collins, whose watching and reporting of International rugby spanned more than half a century, said of him in 1948: 'Geniuses are few. He was one of them. Usually he was a man apart.'

Billy Millar's 1912–13 Springboks were such a powerful side that they had gone through Scotland, Ireland and Wales piling up 57 points without a single point registered against them and looked set to complete the whitewash of the Home Countries in their match against England. But it was Poulton-Palmer who frustrated them with a fantastic run which took him through the defenders from near the right-hand wing towards midfield, back out to the wing again and then infield once more to score under the posts. Millar described it as 'the most magnificent try I have ever seen'.

In 1914 he topped off the last of the Internationals to be played before the outbreak of the Great War by running in four tries against France in Paris.

All that he had done under the name of Poulton. Shortly after the France match he changed it to Poulton-Palmer. He worked for Huntley & Palmers and on the death of his uncle, the Rt. Hon. G. W. Palmer, inherited a fortune – provided that, under the terms of the will, he added Palmer to the Poulton. This done, he joined his regiment, the 4th Royal Berkshires, for service in France.

In the *Centenary History of the Oxford University RFC:* 'He was also an exceptionally good looking young man, which added much to his appeal. But over and above these qualities, Poulton expressed a purity of character which set him apart. It was this extraordinary combination of talents that made him loved by all sorts of men.

'His life ended when he was 25. He was in a trench near Ploegsteert Wood in Belgium; at 12.20 a.m. on 5 May, 1915 he was hit by a sniper's bullet and died without speaking. Captain Crutwell, when writing to his family, said: "When I went round his old Company when they stood to, at dawn, almost every man was crying." '

C. H. 'Cherry' Pillman

Born in January 1890 and educated at Tonbridge, Pillman was said to have 'invented' No. 8 play. One thing certain is that he introduced the technique to South Africans and it was upon him that they based their tradition of bringing that facet of the game to the high levels reached in modern times by such outstanding No. 8s as Muller and Hopwood.

It was while at school, aged 15, that Pillman was taken by his father to Crystal Palace on December 2, 1905, to watch the First All Blacks play New Zealand's first ever International against England. Captaining the All Blacks in the match they were to win comfortably 15–0 was Dave Gallaher, who played 'rover', the forward position completely detached from the 2–3–2 scrum New Zealand used right up until the 1930s. This then quite legal tactic had not been popular with English fans, getting their first taste of it, and the tour had not long been in progress before they were labelling this always loose forward a spoiler and a cheat. Gallaher became such a target for abuse that in a lesser match in London before the International he stood down and let one of the other forwards do the roving job, and remarked wryly, 'I never knew I was so popular', when play constantly interrupted by shouts from the crowd of 'Send that bastard Gallaher off!'

One spectator at the International who did not agree with those sentiments was young Pillman. The effectiveness of a detached forward made a lasting impression upon him and when he left school and joined Blackheath he was determined to emulate his idol. Blackheath, however, would not go along with his suggestion of playing a rover, especially since it came from a teenage newcomer to the club. Nor would they even let him adapt the technique to the 8-man scrum. But such was his brilliance as a player that not only was he snapped up by the selectors for England in 1910 when only just out of his teens. He was allowed full rein as a quick-breaking loose forward and it was mainly through his youthful expertise up front combined with the Stoop genius in the backs that England were to go through the season unbeaten and win their first International Championship for eighteen years. And within weeks he was in the party of thirty of the British Isles on board ship for the new tour of South Africa.

What he did on that tour is now legendary as far as South Africans are concerned. Their rugby historians still refer to it as 'Pillman's Tour'. Reg Sweet in *Pride of the Lions* wrote: 'It is open to question whether any player who came to South Africa has ever matched Cherry Pillman for the starkness of the impact he created. He was the first of the out-and-out breakaways seen in South Africa.' Billy Millar, contemporary captain of the Springboks, wrote in the South African Rugby Board's official history: 'The incomparable

D

Pillman I consider the greatest wing-forward of all time. He revolutionised our ideas of forward play for, with his exceptional pace, he broke away quickly from the scrums to support his backs on attack and also stifled and wrecked attempts by our backs to start movements.' And from an anyonymous South African rugby reporter: 'He played a game apparently invented by himself.'

Not content with having the South Africans reaching for superlatives with his forward play, Pillman ran the risk of coming an awful cropper by playing at fly-half – a role he had never undertaken before – in the third Test. Outcome: the Lions recorded their first and only Test victory against South Africa or New Zealand in the first quarter of this century. And the man responsible for their 8–3 win through engineering both the tries and converting one of them? Bill Millar wrote many years later: 'My memories of the match are all dwarfed by Pillman's outstanding brilliance. He gave the impression that he had never in his life played anywhere but at stand-off half. If ever a man can have been said to have won an international match through his own unorthodox and single-handed efforts, it can be said of the inspired, black-haired Pillman I played against on the Crusaders Ground that day.'

And to cap it all Pillman finished the tour well and truly at the top of of the individual points table with 6T, 17C, 3P and 1D.

All this from the 20-year-old 'baby' of the side!

He returned to be a key man in the England side henceforth, although unfortunately after 18 caps his career ended rather abruptly when he was called from the Reserve of the the Dragoon Guards to serve in the Great War. Undoubtedly if it had not been for that interruption to his rugby when he was only 24 he would have set a much higher most-capped target for England players to chase than Wakefield did in 1927.

After the war it was too late for him to resume for England, and his main attentions were turned to getting Blackheath back into action following the shocking toll which that war had taken of England's young men of military (and rugby) age.

1920s

W. W. Wakefield

Wakefield has always been acknowledged as the greatest forward England has ever produced. One wonders, half a century after his rugby career ended, whether there is any firm reason for questioning this. Another forward, Budge Rogers, was to break his long-standing record for England appearances. But in years to come will old-timers say 'Ah, Rogers! with the same sense of awe accorded Wakefield?

Born in 1898, 'Wakers' was a Sedbergh schoolboy when war broke out and ended it in the RAF, staying on in the service until 1923. In his rugby career through Sedbergh, the RAF, Cambridge University, Harlequins and Middlesex he was invariably captain.

J. B. G. Thomas, in one of his balloon ascensions into rugby hyperbole, wrote of him: 'He could handle like a three-quarter, run like a wing, dribble better than most first-class soccer players, and tackle like an octopus.' Need one add more? Except perhaps to make the comment that the dribbling which was one of his great assets wouldn't cut much ice today, the All Blacks having taught us that it is much smarter to pick the ball up, on the basis that when the ball is at your feet you only have an option on it but when it's in your hands it's yours.

There was no doubt about how fast he was, in view of the fact that he had been RAF champion at that most demanding test of pace for the runner – the 440 – but over and above the basic skills of a loose forward with which he was so well endowed he was a player of thought, an innovator, and a great leader. It was he who took the then emerging style of back-row play on attack and defence, and developed into the technique we know today. As pack leader under the captaincy of W. J. A. Davies and then taking over when the great fly-half retired, Wakefield can be regarded as the key man in England's Golden Era in the early 1920s.

Tommy Voyce

A loose forward in the full sense of the term, Voyce was once accused of being a 'leaner', never lending all his weight to the scrum, to which he indignantly replied: 'I do! When play is in front of the selectors' box.'

He was one of those who enliven the game from time to time – a character. England supporters called him the 'Happy Warrior', as with his sleeves rolled up and an almost perpetual smile on his face he used to pile in. In other camps he was known as the 'Grinning Menace'. He was regarded by many as a dirty player, by his admirers as 'robust'. He and Jammy Clinch, another notably robust performer, carried on a vendetta whenever England and Ireland met. But on one occasion when a referee hastened towards them to suggest they cool it as they were locked in battle some distance from the ball, his warning fell a bit flat as they broke into laughter.

As part of the famous back-row trio of the early 1920s with Wakefield and Blakiston, Voyce always played open-side flanker and had tremendous speed which he used on attack for positioning himself either in support of the back-line or in judicious anticipation of a good spot to head for if there was a tactical kick ahead. In defence he was a sort of 'sweeping spoiler', the moment the ball was out on the opposite setting off at full tilt at the scrum-half, then to the fly-half and eventually the centre, if he hadn't already nailed one of the first two.

His headlong desire to be in the thick of the fray at all times was all the more commendable when one considers that he had only one effective eye.

He was born in 1897 and volunteered at 17 when war broke out and it was during service on the Western Front with the Gloucestershire Regiment that he received the serious eye injury. After the war he was a great favourite at Kingholm in those days when Gloucester was an attractive town. He captained not only the club but also the county and from his début for England in 1920 went through to 27 caps.

He was a shining star in an otherwise lack-lustre Lions side in South Africa, being second in the list of try-scorers and topping the individual points. On the field on that tour he showed his versatility by filling in as full-back, centre and wing, as well as his normal duties as wing-forward. Off the field he was highly applauded for a wonderful sprint – up the corridors of a train in which the team was travelling, to get the engine driver to stop because fire had broken out in their carriage, and, not being able to make himself heard above the noise of the train, getting his attention by throwing coal at him.

Back from South Africa, where one draw was the best the Lions had been able to achieve in the Test series, Voyce's next encourter with the overseas rivals was in the England-New Zealand clash in 1925. It was the match, of course, in which Cyril Brownlie was sent off and not only New Zealanders but also more than a few Englishmen felt the decision was a bit harsh. Those in the know will tell you today that before the match in the England dressing-room there was talk of settling old scores with Brownlie, following incidents in provincial matches during the run-up to the International. Among those seen to be rolling his sleeves up with more than usual relish was Voyce.

Be that as it may, Voyce was to become a valued administrator for English rugby after his retirement from the field of battle in 1927. A long-time member of the R.F.U. Committee, he was elected President in 1960–61 and when in 1970 the rules of the Committee stipulated that he could no longer serve he was co-opted for a further year so that he could complete half a century of service to the R.F.U. as player and official.

Kershaw and Davies

There is no question at all that Kershaw and Davies were the greatest half-back combination England has ever produced. There could be a case for saying that they were the best pairing of any country. If statistics are a yardstick, it is certain that no other country can point to a pair of half-backs who played 14 Internationals together and were never on the losing side.

It is interesting that W. J. A. Davies, born in 1890, was 29 and one might have thought headed for retirement before he even took the field beside Kershaw for their first England outing as a partnership. In fact it had been a toss-up whether they would ever play International rugby on the same side. The youthful 'Dave', playing at fly-half for the Navy and Hampshire, had caught the eye of the Welsh selectors in 1913 and was offered a Trial. He turned them down, to make his début that year for England against the touring Springboks, a match that was lost, to be followed by 21 more appearances for England in the course of which he never came off the field with a beaten team.

The war, in which he served in *Iron Duke* in the Grand Fleet, made a six-year gap in his rugby career and it also delayed the début of scrum-half C. A. ('K') Kershaw, born 1895, a submariner in the Baltic before joining Davies in the first post-war International, England v. Wales, in 1920.

Kershaw was an outstanding fencer, representing England in the sabre and foil in the 1920 Antwerp Olympics, and this had much to do with developing the arm muscles which helped him to hurl the ball at terrific speed to the dapper, long-striding Davies, who would stand 20 yards away between the opposing fly-half and inside centre and draw both of them as he ran forward.

Kershaw was the epitome of an attacking scrum-half, very fast from the base of the scrum, a constant danger when linking with the then newly developing back-row breakaways, in the persons of Wakefield, Voyce and Blakiston. Davies wrote of him: 'In four consecutive years of first class football I doubt whether he ever kicked the ball more than a dozen times.'

Davies himself often did have to resort to kicking, forced upon him by the fast breaking back-row men of opposing sides who were trying to emulate the pioneering England trio, but he never brought it to the extreme which a decade later Bennie Osler did for the Springboks. If he had, the name of Davies would have come down through rugby history coupled in unpopularity with that of the touchline-stitching Osler. Davies, who was to captain England in the last half of his 22 caps and through their Golden Era, was one of the most graceful (left-footed) drop-kickers, on more than one occasion frustrating the opposition with a last minute match-winner.

Kershaw once said that you could forget any idea about

their combination being 'a natural'. 'It didn't just happen,' he recalled in 1967, the year his erstwhile partner died. 'It was bloody hard work. We practised four, often five, nights a week at the Portsmouth United Services ground. We worked up an instinctive co-operation. If I got the ball in a game, no matter where I went, I knew that if I tossed it into the air Dave would be there.'

1930s

H. G. 'Tuppy' Owen-Smith

In the 1930s, a rather arid decade as regards England producing outstanding players, one man stood out as a star shining above his contemporaries. Full-back Owen-Smith, Test cricketer and welter-weight boxer, rivalled C. B. Fry as an all-round sportsman but it would hardly be accurate to say that England produced him. He was a South African whom the England selectors latched on to thankfully when he just happened to be resident in this country in his rugby prime.

1950s

Peter Jackson

Born in 1930 and educated at King Edward VI H.S. in Birmingham, Jackson must be rated as England's greatest three-quarter in the post-war era – unless, after this appears, David Duckham has sufficiently added to his laurels to take the title away from him. But even if Duckham does finish his career in a blaze of glory I think Jackson must have the edge on him for this particular reason: both were wonderfully exciting players, calculated to fill any crowd with instant expectancy whenever they got the ball, but Jackson was far more of a participator and therefore of more value to any side for whom he played. By this I mean that Jackson looked for work all the time; Duckham tended to be the sort of wing who waited for the ball to come to him, and if it didn't he was likely to wind up playing a non-match through being 'starved'. (In this connection, for those who saw the New Zealand wings Grant Batty, the busy competitor, and Bryan

Williams playing in the same game, they exemplified exactly what I am saying.)

The interesting thing, if one continues the Jackson-Duckham comparison is that each started his career in midfield and then was switched to the wing – Jackson taking some of his midfield experience with him and Duckham apparently not so much.

Jackson started – with his school's Old Boys before joining Coventry – as a fly-half but, as he cheerfully remarks, he was so selfish that they moved him out to the wing. But singleness of purpose can be another term for selfishness and Jackson always had the avowed determination to run through the whole side. 'When put in possession,' he said during his playing days, 'I must get to the line and beat the opposition on the way. My feeling towards the game at all times has been to keep the ball in play and run with it rather than letting it get into touch.' He kept this philosophy when banished to the wing. He appeared to have a deep-felt hatred for the touchline, which gave rise to a characteristic of his play for which the fans loved him – setting off inland rather than let himself be forced into touch as so many unimaginative wings allow themselves to be.

This Jackson trade mark was never more in evidence than in a try he scored for the 1959 Lions in the opening match of their tour of New Zealand, against Hawke's Bay. His zig-zag course from touch across to the other wing's side of the goal line appeared to involve every member of the local side in efforts to tackle him and the 52–12 drubbing they got meant nothing to the Hawke's Bay fans if it was going to be inflicted on them with such wonderful stuff as that. News spread throughout New Zealand – just wait till you see this Peter Jackson! And he didn't let them down, his sixteen tries just being pipped by one for the record by Tony O'Reilly, who at the end of the tour was self-effacing enough to say that although he may have been the record-breaker there was no question as to who was the great crowd-pleaser as far as the New Zealand fans were concerned. (See the famous O'Reilly quote on the subject in the Chapter 'The Lions' Share'.)

Jackson's try in the final Test of that 1959 tour had been

even better than his opener, for it was far more important, contributing the winning margin in the Lions' then historic 9–6 victory – the first win they had had over New Zealand for more than half a century. O'Reilly had got things going when he moved into the line from the blind side wing and, finding his way blocked as the passing movement got under way, he threw out a long pass to Ken Scotland at outside centre. Scotland transferred to Jackson 35 yards out with the All Black defence converging on him. Jackson left his opposite number, Caulton, standing with a beautiful side-step and then when McPhail, coming over at top speed from the other wing bore down upon him he swerved past him. Still between Jackson and the line, however, was the formidable figure of Don Clarke. Jackson feinted to go infield and Clarke, knowing the Jackson liking for avoiding the clutches of the touchline, fell for it. He moved just that fraction infield for Jackson to squeeze through the narrow gap he left between himself and the corner flag.

Pale-faced Jackson, whose complexion was so pallid that lying injured on the field people were likely to think he was dead, had scored another sensational try in the previous season against Australia at Twickenham, which I describe in the chapter on rugby's H.Q. and which Jackson on his retirement regarded as the greatest moment of his career.

Another Jackson thriller was the try he made for England against Wales in Cardiff in 1963 which prompted J. B. G. Thomas to write that 'followers of the game, particularly those Welshmen who saw it, regard him as the wing of the decade'. This struck me as very open-minded of the Welsh in view of the fact that their own Stuart Watkins was of the same decade. But on checking I found that that statement had been made in 1963. Watkins made his début in 1964.

Butterfield & Davies

In recent years England fans had great hopes that in Duckham & Spencer they at last had a centre pairing worthy of the name. But then Spencer fell out of favour with the selectors and that was that. Everyone had to go back to bemoaning the fact there hadn't been a really good pair since Butterfield and Davies.

They *were* good. Butterfield was the smaller (5 ft. 11 in., 12 st. 8 lb.), tactical dodgy one. Davies the bigger (6 ft., 13 st. 6 lb.), forceful, penetrating runner. For New Zealanders who saw them in action they were typical of the New Zealand system of the inside centre (second five-eighth) being an opportunity-maker – a second-string fly-half, as it were – for the outside centre (called merely 'the centre' in the New Zealand line-up of backs) to do the powerful running. Conscious that with the five-eighth system they have a much better set-up, New Zealanders are only unhappy that in modern times they have never been able to produce backs of sufficient quality to exploit it to the full. They would have loved to have had Butterfield and Davies working behind their forwards.

The South Africans were similarly impressed when the English pair went out there with the Lions in 1955. With Jeeps and Cliff Morgan inside them and O'Reilly on the right-wing they were devastating, and O'Reilly was the first to acknowledge the debt he owed them in the piling up of his record 16 tries on tour. They were among the stars of the first three Tests in which for the first time this century the Lions had the Springboks going to the final Test 2–1 down and being in the unfamiliar situation of having to win that last one to save their skins. Unaccountably Manager Jack Siggins dropped Davies for this vital match – news that was received with whoops of joy in the Springbok camp – and although it might be unfair to Siggins to say that this strange decision was necessarily the direct cause of South Africa coming out winners 22–8, it could well have been.

R. E. G. (Dickie) Jeeps

Born in 1931 and educated at Bedford Modern, Jeeps became not only far and away his country's best scrum-half in the post-war era. He is a candidate for the title of the best scrum-half England has ever had. Whether Kershaw of the great Kershaw and Davies combination at the beginning of the 1920s was better is something that could have been judged from personal observation by what is by now only a small band of rugby enthusiasts. One thing we know for certain is that with 24 appearances Jeeps is the most capped scrum-half.

And the interesting thing is that at the start of his career, playing for Northampton, he was not recognised by the England selectors. His début in international rugby was for the Lions in South Africa in 1955. And even though he had an outstanding tour, being preferred over the other two scrum-halves on the trip for all four Tests, still the selectors at home were not convinced. On his return they picked him for the first International of the 1955–56 season and then dropped him for the rest. It was only in the following season that he was able to establish himself in their eyes, and at length to be appointed captain of England for the majority of his appearances including leading them to a Triple Crown in 1960.

Jeeps had a distinguished Lions career. (As a matter of interest, Kershaw never played for the British Isles, not being able to get leave from the Navy.) Jeeps established a double record of three tours (1955 in South Africa, 1959 in Australiasia and 1962 again in South Africa) and 13 Test appearances, only excelled by McBride on the 1974 tour to South Africa.

Jeeps played on drier grounds out there. My main remembrance of him here was that it always seemed to be muddy (did we have more rain in those days?), in conditions in which untidy line-outs, endless mêlées and pursuit of the soapy ball can make life a misery for a scrum-half. But the stocky, tough as nails, mud-soaked figure of Jeeps was always seen bouncing back after concentrated pummelling by line-out forwards breaking through and flankers on the rampage.

On defence there was no other scrum-half to compare with him. In attack he did perhaps tend to play rather much close to the pack, but he was in that period prior to restricted kicking to touch and the 4-point try that was not generally noted for open back play. He was not a flashy player but whom do we remember now of his contemporaries who were more showy?

His final rugby achievement was to be appointed, when just into his 30s, to the Committee of the R.F.U., where the average age must surely be at least 20 years more, and this was regarded as a great step forward in what has been described as a game run by old men for young men to play.

Marques and Currie

The greatest pair of locks England has ever had, Marques and Currie made 22 consecutive International appearances together – a record not only for that combination but one is hard put to it to think of any partnership elsewhere in the field which has equalled this. Centres Butterfield and Davies, for example, had precisely half the number of outings together.

Marques and Currie were described as chalk and cheese – Marques the showy one, Currie the stolid grafter. This worked to their advantage, since time and again when they took the field the watchword in the enemy camp was 'Mark Marques!' With all the attention focused on his partner, Currie was able to get away with all sorts of things – even if poor Marques came in for more of a pounding then he would have wished.

David Marques was born in Hertfordshire in 1932 of an Australian father and a Welsh mother, which sounds like a good enough qualification for England. He went to Tonbridge and was at school with Colin Cowdrey. They played in the same XV, Cowdrey showing great talent as a fly-half until unfortunately he had to be dropped. He got too fat. In passing it is interesting that of these two contemporaries at Tonbridge, Marques has been retired from rugby for more than a decade as I write this, with a newspaper on my desk proclaiming that yesterday Cowdrey scored as good a ton as he has ever knocked up.

Marques went on to Cambridge, where in his four Varsity matches he was opposed by John ('Muscles') Currie, born in Clifton, also in 1932, and an Old Boy of Bristol Grammar School. They wound up all square in their 1954–57 encounters, Cambridge winning two, Oxford two.

They linked for the first time when they joined Harlequins in the 1955–56 season and in a matter of months were latched on to by the England selectors for their joint début against Wales in what now seem those far-off days when reputations were established at Oxbridge which were the open-seasame to caps for England.

Marques and Currie were tremendous jumpers in the line-out – unaided by the lift-up technique brought to such a high pitch of efficiency by the Springboks that one might think it was legal, so rarely is it punished by referees. So spectacular were the leaps of the English pair that they were the joy of the press photographers, giving a new dimension to that traditional line-out shot which, let's face it, can be more than a little boring.

So high did Marques in particular jump that in one match against Ireland his marker despaired of getting anything like his height and became so frustrated that at one line-out he decided that the only way to counter Marques as he went up was, as it were, to grab a handful. Returning to earth after delivering the ball to his scrum-half, Marques turned to the Irishman and enquired: 'Are you trying to prove something?'

1960s

Richard Sharp

Born in Mysore, Southern India, in 1938, the 6 ft. 12 st. Sharp was the most exciting England player to emerge in the post-war era. Educated at Blundell's, that good rugby nursery in Devon, and Balliol, Oxford, he was three times in the Varsity match, making his sensational début for England in the middle year (see chapter on Twickenham). Old-timers had to think back for a long time before they could recall anyone who had occupied the fly-half slot for England with such flair.

Not a jinker or side-stepper of the Cliff Morgan or Phil Bennett type, his forte was the graceful, effortless swerving around an opponent, mesmerised, not quite knowing when to make the tackle and then, when the decision was reached, Sharp was in the clear.

He was also one of the masters of the dummy. (Not *the* master. That was a man named McKeogh in the early days of New Zealand rugby whose dummy was so devastating that on one occasion when he threw one at the opposing full-back to go across for a try he not only hoodwinked the full-back but also the referee, who whistled him up for a forward pass.) Sharp's most famous exploitation of the dummy was when, as described elsewhere in this book, he scored a spectacular match-winning try against Scotland after three in succession.

Inevitably a time comes when it is felt that as penetrating a fly-half as Sharp must be stopped at all costs, and preferably be removed from rugby for some time, not just for the remainder of the current match. Thus it was that with the Lions in South Africa in 1962 Sharp found himself hospitalised for weeks following a late tackle by Mannie Roux so vicious that it was regarded by those who witnessed it as one of the blackest moments of international rugby.

Sharp wrote his life story, *Winning Rugby,* and everybody expected that he would have much to say about that incident. Instead he dismissed it with a couple of sentences, which only went to prove what a different type of person he is from the diminutive Mr Roux.

A pity that Sharp's rugby career was to end on a downbeat. He was brought out of retirement in 1967 to captain England against Australia. Granted at that time England were in dire straits for a fly-half of quality but it was an unfortunate rush of blood to the head on the part of the selectors to ask Sharp to don his International boots again four years after he had wisely decided to quit while he was ahead, as Americans aptly put it. No matter. The fans of his era put that one from their minds, to keep fresh in memory the great enjoyment and excitement his presence on a rugby field had brought them.

Sharp teaches geography at Sherborne School in Dorset, which could be a contributing reason why so many boys want to go there and why it is one of the few English Public Schools today with a waiting list.

Bob Hiller

Born in 1942 and educated at Bec School, Birmingham University and Oxford (where he was a Double Blue), Hiller was to wind up his International career as a controversial figure. But in a country not noted for producing outstanding full-backs with long tenure of office there is no question that he rates.

He was from the same mould as New Zealand's Bob Scott, i.e. a running-around, joining-in sort of full-back (at the Middlesex Sevens for Harlequins there were few more energetic) and he was as capable as Scott of winning matches with his boot from the standing ball or the dropped one. There were times when he was called upon to do all England's scoring, as in 1971 when he immediately followed his single-handed beating of Ireland through three penalties (9–6) by supplying all 14 of England's points with a try, conversion and three penalties in the draw with France. (*Note:* Although he overlapped into the 1970s I list him in the 1960s since it was at the close of that decade that he came into his prime, including the achieving of something which no other England captain had ever managed before.)

Hiller established a world record with his kicking in 1968 with the Lions in South Africa, when he scored the quickest ever century on an international tour, totalling 104 in a mere eight matches, thus beating Don Clarke's 'ton' in nine matches for the All Blacks in Australia in 1962. He proved his worth to any side, on tour or otherwise, by recording another century (in ten matches) on the 1971 Lions tour of Australia and New Zealand.

There were some, even among his most ardent followers, who became impatient with the time he took to tee up his place-kicks, but those of his fans who were critical would abruptly switch to being highly pleased when one of his siege-gun efforts would sail between the post to change the whole complexion of a match.

He was inclined to be a bit too chatty – especially at the top of his voice when trying to captain teams from the remoteness of full-back. But the thing was that he was colourful – a constant focal point of interest on and off the field. And in the latter regard he was shabbily treated by the England selectors in the 1969–70 season.

Before the England team was even picked for the first of that season's five Internationals, against South Africa on December 20, 1969, Hiller was announced as captain for all the matches. It was hailed as a splendid idea, following the precedent of some other countries and also common in cricket. Hiller, secure in his job, would not have the axe hanging over him and could concentrate on team-building around him – or rather in front of him. And it at once paid dividends. In that opening International of the season he became the first England captain to lead his side to victory against the Springboks, after more than 60 years of trying.

Hiller then went on to beat Ireland in the first of the Home Internationals with the two magnificent dropped goals which gave England their 9–3 win. Wales snatched victory from England in the next match, thanks to the game of his career played by Chico Hopkins as replacement for Gareth Edwards. And then a lively Scotland pack got the better of England. And what did the selectors do for the final International, against France? They dropped Hiller.

As one rugby writer put it, 'Hiller's fate was the most discussed topic in clubhouses up and down the country.' Apart from the fact that on balance he could be far from discredited for losing two and winning two (one of them the historic defeat of South Africa), the discussions hinged on this aspect: it was a definite breach of contract by the selectors. How could any England player in future have confidence in any assurances given him by his bosses, the selectors?

In the event England without Hiller were thoroughly lambasted by France, who piled up 35 points, the most ever scored by them against any of the Home Countries since they had entered the Championship in 1906. This provided a certain solace for Hiller, although he and the England supporters would have much preferred that the situation which brought such solace had never arisen in the first place.

A lineout during the England v. New Zealand match at Twickenham in January 1925 . . .

. . . and during the England v. New Zealand match in 1967

Richard Sharp, one of the outstanding English players of the 1960s

Alan Old, England fly-half and British Lion, pictured during the England v. Wales match at Twickenham in March, 1974

Dickie Jeeps, probably the best scrum-half to play for England since the war, pictured playing for the British Lions against Hawkes Bay during the New Zealand tour of 1959

R. W. D. Marques, shown here winning the ball at a lineout, a leading English forward between 1956 and 1961

Knickers at Twickers: The great W. W. Wakefield, pictured with referee Tommy Vile at the England v. Scotland fixture in 1924

1970s

In trying to assess which players of the early 1970s are likely to graduate as English greats of all time it is perhaps best to imagine that it is 1980 and we are looking back over the decade.

From that vantage point one would undoubtedly say that John Pullin was an outstanding hooker and successful captain – notably against South Africa and New Zealand on their home territory. But counting against him, perhaps unfairly, is that his career should have ended on a high note but didn't. Regarded as a certainty for his third Lions tour, to South Africa in 1974, he was the surprise omission, his place going to fledgeling R. W. Windsor, of Wales, whom the front-row experts felt had completely outhooked him in the England-Wales International just prior to selection of the touring side.

England's pack of the early 1970s was her best for a long time, as witness far more of them being chosen for the 1974 Lions tour of South Africa – six – than from the other Home Countries. Fran Cotton, Mike Burton and Stack Stevens alternating in support of Pullin in the front row; Ralston and Uttley the locks; Neary and Dixon flankers; Ripley No. 8. Well drilled and effective, but how many, if any, would individually graduate into the Greats?

The England fans loved Andy Ripley. Six feet five of him, long-striding, hair flowing in the breeze, galloping for the line was something they thrilled to. Just wait till he gets to South Africa with the Lions, they said, what a hit he'll be with the crowds there. But it didn't quite work out that way. Roger Uttley, converted from lock to flanker, was the one who got a regular Test place on tour as a loose forward.

Of the others in the pack time alone will tell how large they loom for future generations.

As to England's backs of the early 1970s . . . Nothing outstanding at full-back or scrum-half. Squires on the wing, Evans at centre and Alan Old at fly-half – not bad but doubtful to be regarded as world-beaters when eventually their careers were over. Only one back, unavailable for the 1974 Lions tour, could be looked upon as a strong candidate for a place among the all-time greats.

David Duckham

Duckham was born in 1946 and went to King Henry VIII Grammar School in Coventry before becoming a bank clerk. He graduated from rugby for Coventry and Warwickshire to hit the big time with a flourish in the last year of the 1960s – England cap, Barbarians, Lions all in the space of his début year, 1969. He had burst forth upon an appreciative English public as a centre, with Cambridge man John Spencer as his running mate. And everybody sat back and said how wonderful it was that at last England had a pair of centres worthy of the name, after the long bleak period since Butterfield and Davies in the 1950s. But it was short-lived. Spencer fell by the wayside after just a couple of seasons and it was decided to turn Duckham into a wing, a switch which many were to feel was never quite 100 per cent satisfactory.

Be that as it may, there was no doubt that David Duckham was possessed of charisma – that vogue word that has just found its way into the dictionaries, 'divine gift or talent, capacity to inspire followers with devotion and enthusiasm'. And what numbers him among the greats is that every time the ball came into his possession there was an instant upsurge of excitement throughout the crowd (excitement tinged with apprehension if you were supporting his opponents) and there would be a wonderful feeling of expectancy as he set off on one of his runs. Even if there wasn't a try at the end of it his crashing speed and devastating side-step gave you your money's worth. And when he did go over for a try invariably it was a classic, the sort you just can't wait to get home after the match to savour again on TV's Rugby Special.

And finally, on the subject of Greats, to indulge in something that is always interesting to do and to pick holes in when someone else does it – choosing an All-time XV.

To take the whole range of England players from Victorian to modern times is not really very practical because (a) there are invariably so many outstanding candidates for any key position – scrum-half, say – that men with obvious claims to the job have to be passed over because you need only one, and (b) there aren't many people around now who saw Stoop, for instance, or Poulton-Palmer in action, so what genuine yardstick is there for comparing them with modern players? Therefore, let us restrict ourselves to those whom a great number of rugby followers know at first hand – the England players who have been in action since World War II.

And so we dive in at the deep end with:

ENGLAND POST-WAR XV

Full-back: Bob Hiller (Harlequins) 1968–72
Wings: Peter Jackson (Coventry) 1956–63; David Duckham (Coventry) 1969–
Centres: Jeff Butterfield (Northampton) 1953–59; W. P. C. Davies (Harlequins) 1953–58
Fly-half: Richard Sharp (Oxford) 1960–67
Scrum-half: Dickie Jeeps (Northampton, capt.) 1956–62
No. 8: Andy Ripley (Rosslyn Park) 1972–
Flankers: Budge Rogers (Bedford) 1961–69; Peter Robbins (Oxford) 1956–62
Locks: R. W. D. Marques (Harlequins) 1956–61; J. D. Currie (Bristol) 1956–62
Props: Fran Cotton (Loughborough Colls) 1971–; C. R. Jacobs (Northampton) 1956–64
Hooker: Eric Evans (Sale) 1948–58

One observes that of the two full decades in this post-war era – the 1950s and the 1960s – the former contribute nine of the team and the latter merely three. Does that mean that in the 1950s England were three times better than they were in the 1960s? Checking on how many times they won the International Championship in each decade, it would seem to be so. In the 1950s they were outright champions three times and in the 1960s only once. Over-simplification perhaps, but interesting nevertheless.

13. *When the War Was Over*

I don't know about you, but as far as life in general was concerned I felt that the 1950s were the dreariest decade I've ever had to get through. Austerity and wartime controls still around, sweets and clothing still rationed. Everything and everybody looked drab. Beer had not yet recovered from the serious case of anaemia it had contracted during the war and whisky might just have well have been rationed considering how difficult it was to buy a bottle. And on top of it all there was a Labour Government, which is enough to do serious damage to any decade.

But, thank goodness, organised sport was back and how everybody flocked to the stadiums after having been starved for it through all those war years. I remember that for county championship cricket matches, now played out invariably with more people on the field than in the stands, the crowds were such that overflow had to be accommodated on the grass at Lords even for things like Middlesex v. Kent.

They had got big time rugby going again right after the war with a tour by the New Zealand Services team, the Kiwis, who joined with the Home Countries and France in a series of Victory Tests. And then when the Championship proper got under way once more it was to be dominated by Ireland, thanks mainly to a great pack of forwards and the superb Jackie Kyle.

It might have been argued that naturally the Irish were in a position to be strong, since the Republic of Ireland had been neutral during the hostilities and therefore did not suffer to the same extent as the others. But this argument didn't really hold water when one considers that the next country to make an impact on the International scene was one that had really suffered. In 1951 France reached a rugby milestone by beating England at Twickenham for the first time since starting her visits there in 1911.

Even better was to come for France before the decade was out. Inspired by the great Jean Prat, she took a share of the Championship for the first time in 1954 (with England and Wales), won jointly with Wales in the following season and then broke her duck by winning it outright in 1959. By then the French were under the leadership of Lucien ('Voice of Thunder') Mias, had such other mighty men in the pack as Celaya, Crauste, Roques and Domenech and behind them as key man in a brilliant back-line Albaladejo – Monsieur le Drop. And having come to the top they decided to stay there, heading the Championship table again in the next three seasons.

In coronation year, 1953, it was felt that everybody in a position to do so should make a grand gesture towards our new Queen and what with Col. Hunt's expedition getting to the top of Everest and England's cricketers winning the Ashes from Australia for the first time in 20 years, the least the rugbymen could do for her was to win the International Championship, something which they hadn't achieved outright since 1937. This they duly did with a fine unbeaten run, soundly disposing of Scotland, Wales and France and drawing with Ireland.

Captain that season was Nim Hall, a great warhorse for England – fly-half, centre, full-back, place-kicker and captain for all of his 17 caps except the first four. On the right wing was another great favourite with the crowds, the 14-stone butcher Ted Woodward, not the least reason why he was so popular being that it was a wonderful sight to see, a man so big powering his way along the touchline.

England carried on the good work in the next season and won the Triple Crown, but not oddly enough the outright Championship which usually goes with it. It was a rare freak of the Five-nations tournament that the Triple Crown winner shared the title with two others (France and Wales).

But in 1957 and 1958 they were back again as outright winners.

Besides Hall and Woodward, main contributors to these good deeds were centres Butterfield and Davies and Peter Jackson and forwards Eric Evans and Don White, the 23 times capped Oxford captain John Kendall-Carpenter and that outstanding combination at lock, Marques & Currie.

It all sounds very good but let us confess that much of the International rugby of this period and over into the beginning of the 1960s was very dull indeed. One indication of this was in the 1959 season England did not score a single try. Main reason and the bugbear of rugby at this time – defensive football.

The habit had developed of the backline of a team, unless within something like striking distance of the line, lying right up flat. This meant that the side on attack, gaining possession from scrum or line-out, found that their backs were almost invariably stifled. The fly-halves of this period did a lot of kicking, not by choice as with Bennie Osler in the 1930s and then later by other men in that slot who imagined themselves at tactical kicking. In the late 1950s and early 60s the fly-half so often had no option but to kick – rather than send on to his colleagues each with his opposite number right on top of him.

(In passing it is worth noting that it was in this period that New Zealand developed the technique of 'second phase play', with which she was to have such great success around the world. New Zealand rugby thinkers reasoned this way: The way defensive football has become so dominant it is now almost impossible to score from a set piece. Therefore, gaining possession from a set piece we will manufacture another situation elsewhere – the second phase – and getting possession from that ruck the defence will not be all lined up against us and we will have a scoring opportunity.)

Meanwhile, back at the ranch . . . Much credit is due to the International Rugby Board who, unlike the powers-that-be in soccer today, decided something really must be done about the impasse, and they did it.

Reason for my allusion to soccer is that as we were approaching the mid-point of the 70s soccer – as a game –

was in a terrible state. I refer to the Art of Chopping, which had been brought to its peak. A defender, confronted with someone breaking through with the ball at his feet, the defence in disarray, what to do about it? Simple. Just chop him. Ruthlessly. Right out there in front of everybody. The referee rushes up, says 'Naughty! Naughty!' Perhaps makes a jotting in his notebook. And what is the outcome? The team which committed the foul does not suffer as in rugby (penalty try). On the contrary they gain all the advantage. They are allowed to bring back all their defenders and line them up between the free-kick taker and the goal. Does that make sense? Soccer as a spectacle and certainly as a game in which to take part was being ruined. And soccer's law-makers have just stood by and let it continue, when a simple solution would be the introduction of a new rule whereby all defenders who were behind the advancing player when the offence was committed must stay there when the kick is taken.

Soccer is a pro game – played and run by professionals – and therefore, one should imagine, better run than rugby, conducted by a bunch of amateurs. It is not so. It is to be highly commended the way the International Board stepped in to frame radically new laws whereby the game would get out of a stalemate and be much more enjoyable for players and spectators alike.

In the 1960s, overlapping into the early 1970s, these were the main law-changes which have contributed to its being the booming sport it is right now:

The Fumble – It had always seemed a bit ridiculous that when, for example, on a muddy day a fly-half received an atrocious pass, juggled with the soapy ball and miraculously managed to hold it he was penalised for his achievement. Even more ridiculous was the sight of officious referees whistling up a player making an adjustment with the ball behind him – how could he have been deemed to have 'thrown forward' backwards? Thankfully the law was changed to permit legitimate adjustment and the whistle-happy referees were curbed, to the all-round benefit of the flow of play.

A Yard Apart in the Line-Outs – The line-out, with its

difficulty of avoiding a mess of bodies, has long been one of the main traffic jams of rugby. Rugby League got around the problem by abandoning it altogether and instead getting the two sets of forwards to bunch up together against each other, a scrum-half to throw the ball at them, catch it again and run off with it – laughingly called a scrum. Senior readers will remember that in rugby in the old days the side with the throw-in had the option of taking a scrum. This applied up until the last war. But it had been felt that it gave an advantage to the team with the bigger pack – especially the massive Springbok forwards of the 1930s who had no trouble at all in pushing anything in front of them off the ball. In 1937 Scotland suggested that the scrum option should be scrapped and it was put before the four Home Unions to decide. Two years later a decision was arrived at. So was the war. It was not until 1946 that the International Board could confirm that henceforth the ball in touch called only for a line-out. And despite its shortcomings this characteristic feature of the game had been persevered with. There have been numerous modifications over the years. The latest, the spacing of a yard between the two lines, has cleaned it up to a degree.

Substitutes – Examples of great matches being ruined through injuries making them no longer a contest between two teams of 15 players were so numerous that they need no detailing here. It is interesting that the fears of the reactionaries who held out so long against replacements that it would lead to abuse have proved quite unfounded. The pro-substitute camp always argued that no rugby player, unless in really bad shape, would want or would permit himself to be yanked from the field at the height of a game. And with the introduction of 'reserves' in 1969 it has proved that way – never a hint of any team indulging in sharp practice in this regard. Allowed at first merely in Internationals and in matches played against overseas touring sides, it was inevitable that there would be agitation to have it extended to lower levels. At least one of the R.F.U.'s Club Knock-out finals had been rendered a non-contest by the departure from the field at an early stage of a key man, a hooker. The International Board were wise enough to yield to the pressure.

They said Home Unions could make up their own minds. The Rugby Union did in 1974, when they announced that substitutes would be allowed also in County and Club Knock-out matches. Ordinary club rugby? It's just a matter of time.

Ten Yards Behind the Line-out – The backs (apart from the scrum-half) were forced to retire from the advanced defensive positions they used to occupy at set pieces and the team gaining possession had space in which their backline could manoeuvre. Great!

Four Points for a Try – From the time the method of scoring was standardised in 1905 as a try 3 points, conversion 2, penalty 3, dropped goal 4, there have been only two changes. In 1948 the long-held contention that 4 for a dropped goal was out of proportion saw its reduction to 3. And in the 1971–72 season a try was boosted to 4. Idea behind it: to take the accent off penalties and make teams, for heaven's sake, go for tries. The penalty had got increasingly out of hand since the charging of penalty kicks (as with kicks from marks) was abolished in 1925. And just how out of hand things had got is underlined in red ink by this little statistic:

No. of penalties in International Championship – 1924: 2
No. of penalties in International Championship – 1971: 31

A 1,350 per cent increase! The International Board's bold step in increasing the value of the try has not as yet noticeably lowered the penalty rate (only restitution of the charge or a system of differential penalties will do that) but it *has* added a new dimension to the game. Lagging behind in the closing stages of a match, a teams finds that that 6 points for a converted try is a great stimulus to run the ball, with a real chance of making up what formerly would have seemed hopeless arrears. The 4-point try may not have curbed the penalty takers throughout a match, but we are now getting some cracking good finishes.

Restricted Kicking to Touch – This was the really important one, the rewriting of Law 27 whereby a ball kicked direct into touch meant a line-out from where it was kicked, except when the kicker was in his own 25. In my youth in my native land, playing for Varsity 2B (or was it 4B?), that was the way we used to do it, as everybody else did in New Zealand. Plus the legitimate fumble. Plus substitutes, whom we called 'emergencies', in all levels of rugby (including schools). Whether or not these were dispensations from the International Board I do not know. But I do know that whenever the Lions paid us a visit we quickly switched to British rules and regulations for the matches against them. New Zealand, and Australia, had long pleaded with the Rugby Football Union, when under their aegis, and then with the International Board to make these practices the general rule because they felt – or rather, they *knew* – that it made for a better game. Now they *are* the general rule and everybody's happy.

Footnote: While the International Board is in such an affable mood about law changes, here's another that they might well turn to. The above new laws have all been directed, successfully, to making rugby a more open, free-flowing game. In my youth New Zealand had another domestic law which contributed greatly to open play: at a scrum no player was allowed to advance beyond a line drawn through the centre of the scrummage until the ball was out the other side, i.e. a scrum-half was not allowed to follow the progress of the ball through the opposing pack and pounce on his opposite number as soon as he got it. When the Lions came and New Zealanders had for the time being to play under the British system it annoyed them that so many back movements were in this way killed at birth. The International Board might consider trying out this restriction on marauding scrum-halves. It does wonders for getting the ball out and about among the backs.

In the 1970–71 season the Rugby Football Union laid on elaborate celebrations to mark their centenary, the highlight of which was a match at Twickenham between England and a President's XV of overseas stars – a slightly more public affair than the 1923 centenary match between England-Wales and Scotland-Ireland at the school which was the birthplace of the game.

The President's XV, which played three warm-up games in the provinces before the big match, had all the big rugby names from outside Britain, including New Zealand's Lochore, Meads, Kirkpatrick, Going and Bryan Williams . . . South Africa's Dawie de Villiers, Marais and Du Preez . . . France's Villepreux, Maso and Cester . . . Australia's captain P. G. Johnson, and Barley and Qoro from Fiji.

At Twickenham, with the Queen, the Duke of Edinburgh and Prince Andrew on hand, they played open, nothing-on-the-result football to run away with the match 28–11.

It was wonderful to see such a constellation of stars in action but there were always those who always felt that exhibition rugby is all very well but it lacks the fine edge of the result having a measure of importance. There was a feeling in some quarters that when shortly afterwards the Scottish Rugby Union celebrated their centenary with an international seven-a-side tournament featuring the same sort of star-studded cast (and won to England) the competitive aspect made it a memorable brainwave on the part of the Scots.

After the R.F.U.'s centenary match there was a dinner on a grand scale – 1,000 guests, no less! – at which Prince Philip was the main speaker. Also part of the celebrations was the issue of a 9p stamp, the design beging an adaptation of the painting of a Cambridge-Newport match done by W. B. Wollen and hung on the line at the Royal Academy in 1897. Collectors were able to get a first day cover signed by former England captains and with a special Twickenham postmark. Garter King of Arms approved an R.F.U. coat of arms to mark the occasion. There was a colour film titled 'William Webb Ellis Are You Mad? issued for cinema and TV use. Souvenirs included ties, women's headscarves, Spode chinaware and – biggest seller of them all – centenary tea towels, given in great numbers by rugbymen to wives and girl friends to make them feel, as they used them, that the work they do in the clubhouse kitchen on match days really is appreciated. U. A. Titley, then *Times* rugby writer, and Ross McWhirter, twin-half of the brains behind the *Guinness Book of Records*, produced the *Centenary History of the R.F.U.*, and the rugby writers as a whole gave their services free in bringing out a cracking good paperback, *Touchdown,* which sold like hotcakes.

All that was needed to complete the festivities was for England to win the Championship. Sad to say, they didn't, only missing the Wooden Spoon by a whisker.

14. Where Do We Go From Here?

England shared the Championship with France in 1960 and won it outright in 1963. That they showed up well at the beginning of the 60s was through the good services of Don Rutherford at full-back, Malcolm Phillips and Mike Weston in the centre and those outstanding halves Jeeps and Sharp; Peter Jackson was still going great guns on the right wing; up front there were those two solid front-row gentlemen Jacobs and Judd; Marques and Currie were playing their final matches as England's great lock combination and Budge Rogers in 1961 made the début that was to develop into a record 34 caps.

But within the space of just a couple of years all that was left of these regulars were Rutherford, Judd and Rogers. We were in the era of McFadyean, Bob Lloyd, Finlan, Ashby among others, behind newcomer Pullin and Larter, Owen, Powell, Payne, Treadwell . . . a good name for a forward – Treadwell – but one might well ask now, who's he? England had gone into a phase of not being too good. Nor were Scotland and Ireland. The Championship, from 1965 through to the end of the 60s, became a private affair fought out between Wales (the dazzling Barry John!) and France (Cester & Co.).

A contributing factor to England not doing well could have been that one criticism which can be levelled consistently against England selectors is that they do not appear to have faith in their own selections. Perhaps there are too many of them on the panel. Perhaps it is akin to that scathing observation somebody once made that a camel is a racehorse designed by a committee. To mix the metaphor, perhaps when the coterie of selectors get their heads together to make the final selection, there are so many oars that have to be put in that they rock the boat, not staying to a steady course.

Statistics prove how fickle England's selectors are. Over the years players of the other major rugby nations regularly take over the leadership in their country's list of Leading Cap Winners, gradually lifting it up over the 50 mark – as with Ireland, France and New Zealand. This is an indication that their selectors have confidence in newly chosen players, persist with them.

In England on the other hand such is the chopping and changing that W. W. Wakefield, with his 31 caps accumulated on his retirement in 1927, sat there at the top of the list year after year, generation after generation.

Not wishing to malign Budge Rogers, one must say that it was only the accident of England being short of a worthwhile loose forward in 1969 that he was brought from his personal wilderness as an International and given four caps which boosted him over Wakefield and at long last set a new figure for England of 34, still pitifully behind every other country's leading cap winners.

From 1927 to 1969 – that's 42 years in which England's selectors lacked loyalty towards their choices, while at time of writing Ireland's selectors were capping McBride 52 times, Kiernan 54, Gibson 47, Kyle 46 . . . New Zealand – Meads 55 . . . France – Dauga 70, Spanghero 42 . . . Wales – Ken Jones 44 . . . Scotland – McLeod 40.

One can feel sorry for aspiring young English rugby players. Chosen for England, they have about as much sense of security as an ice cube. For example, young Mike Bulpitt, whom I used to watch playing alongside my elder son at school – a grand total of one consecutive cap for England. His experience can be multiplied by the dozen. How can you prove yourself in one International, when circumstances quite beyond your control may militate against giving a good performance.

At least in England's cricket there is some sort of faith in players chosen. Two shining examples – Amiss and Fletcher, whom the selectors were sure were of the stuff of which Test batsmen are made and who were not banished to the humdrum life of perpetual county cricket after early failures in the Big Time. They were persevered with and eventually faith in them paid dividends when they were mainly the ones who put England on the ascendency . . . until a sheila named Lillian Thomson struck.

But it is probably in the matter of captaincy that England's rugby selectors are at their most capricious. Towards the end of the 1960s a stage was reached whereby England seemed to be having more captains than there were actual International matches. 'How about it, Tom? (Dick? Harry?) Like to be captain against Wales on Saturday?' That, with only slight exaggeration, seemed to be the approach.

Suddenly conscious that that sort of thing didn't make for good cohesion, continuity or morale within a team and also aware of the ridicule from Press and public, the selectors decided in 1970 to be incisive. But as *Punch* wrote of Anthony Eden at the time of the Suez crisis, 'when a ditherer decides to put his foot down he invariably puts it in the wrong place.' Bob Hiller was announced as captain of England for all her Internationals that season. And the shabby outcome of that we have already gone into in the section about Hiller.

However, in 1969 a very important thing happened for England and it was hoped that among other things it would see an end to the inconsistency of the selectors. Having done a violation of the Trade Descriptions Act in 1958 by appointing Don Rutherford a paid 'technical administrator' to the R.F.U., in other words boss of coaching, the Rugby Union came right out with it in 1969 with the appointment of the first ever paid coach for the national side.

He was Don White, likeable former Northampton forward (14 England caps, 1947–52). He was perhaps a bit too affable for a tough job and didn't last long. But the point was that the breakthrough had been made. The casual approach to preparation for Internationals was at an end. England was involved in squad training, drilled by a paid coach. We had entered the phase of 'Christ! I've got to have more match practice, to get in shape for training.'

Team building, which as we have seen appeared to be ot casual interest to the England selectors, now became of prime importance under a paid coach. There were pre-season tours to such places as Canada and the Far East. The squad was kept together so that there was continuity from year to year and although naturally there were changes there was a basic team there that combined well through experience together.

There was a good three-quarter line of Squires-Preece-Evans-Duckham . . . when all were fit. Alan Old at fly-half had his place-kicking to assure his presence in the team. Steve Smith and Jan Webster were sharing the scrum-half slot. Full-back was, granted, something of a problem after the enforced retirement of Bob Hiller. But hadn't producing an outstanding, consistent full-back been a traditional England problem? Over the years some good ones . . . H. T. ('The Octopus') Gamlin, which is going back a bit, Willcox, Rutherford, Hiller. Of world class, though? Even Hiller admitted that on his two Lions tours he was there merely as a member of the 'T and W's', his own expression for tourists who play in just the Tuesday and Wednesday fixtures, never make the Saturday or Test teams.

The forwards, which were the real strength of the side: hooker and captain John Pullin, supported in the front row by Stevens, Cotton and/or Burton; Ralston and Uttley the locks and the back row of Neary, Ripley, Dixon and/or Watkins. It was far and away the best pack in the Championship, and, as mentioned earlier, contributed six to the 1974 Lions forwards.

Great crowd-pleaser of the forwards, and in this respect vying with Duckham in the team as a whole, was Andy Ripley, the best No. 8 England had had for many a long day. Lanky and loose-limbed, he was no mean performer over the hurdles as well as on the rugby field, and just as instant excitement was brought to the crowd whenever Duckham got possession so too did they rise to the sight of Ripley making one of his runs. Swift long strides devouring the ground, as the cliché had it, long flowing from his head-band, he looked like some Indian brave running late on his way to a war dance.

A reason why he was not, as his English fans had expected, a star for the 1974 Lions in their Tests in South Africa (wasn't even in the Test side) was probably a failing he had in regard to the superb breaks he made. When he went all the way, to score, it was great. But when that wasn't the outcome, he did have a tendency to die with the ball. One contributing reason was that he was so bloody fast that often as not none of the other forwards could stay anywhere near him in support and when brought down the advantage of all the yardage he had gained was not really achieved. That was hardly his fault but what was his fault was his incorrect positioning. Although one can be sure that it had been dinned into him, he so frequently ignored the essential that the break must be followed by a successful ruck, the ball carrier creating it in the right position for the ball to come back (leading with one shoulder, ball down at the other side) – *not* with the ball in front of him, to be brought down on top of it and the ruck killed with pile-up, whistle, set scrum.

But Ripley was young and it was felt, hoped, that he would mature into a No. 8 of world class.

We have dealt earlier with the success this basic team was to achieve with wins over South Africa and New Zealand on their own soil in 1972 and 73. The disappointing thing was that such good deeds were not repeated at home. How on earth could a team fresh from an unbeaten tour of South Africa manage to get the Wooden Spoon, losing all their matches, in the Championship? England managed it.

If the 1974 Lions came within an ace of being called the 'Invincibles', England in the same era were undoubtedly the 'Inconsistents'.

England seemed to lack what the Lions had in such good measure – the determination to win, to dominate. This was brought to the point of aggressiveness. After some torrid action at Durban, Tommy Bedford, the Springbok philsopher, missed a glorious opportunity to keep his trap shut when he said: 'In my years as a student at Oxford, and in Britain generally, I enjoyed and saw some of the best rugby of my career outside South Africa. But today I saw another side of British rugby – and I know which I prefer. I think that is enough said on the subject.'

Now wait a minute! I seem to remember Bedford in Springbok teams which were aggressive up to and on many occasions beyond the bounds of 'rugged play' – anything from entering a maul feet-first to crippling late tackles. And he knows from personal experience that the All Blacks can regard rugby as a give-and-take game, in a 75–25 ratio. Did he mean that what was all right for the Springboks and the All Blacks was unbecoming to the British, who must continue to play 'polite' losing rugby?

'Bull' Irvine of the 1924 All Blacks in Britain exemplified the New Zealand approach of establishing psychological superiority over one's opponents at the earliest stage of a match. In a game against an English regional team he flagrantly late tackled one of their forwards and then as they got up Irvine rounded on him: 'What the hell do you think you're doing? You do that again and there'll be trouble.' The bewildered Englishman apologised.

The All Blacks were still using that approach in 1967 when Colin Meads in one of the Internationals said to his opposite number in the first line-out: 'I'm going to grind your face in the mud and, etc., etc.' When the player was asked after the match what *he* said to Meads he replied: 'I said "F*** off". But not very loud.'

As the Americans say, nice guys come second. And this can apply in work as well as sport. In the newspaper world there is a saying – Fleet Street is full of nice ex-editors.

Not for one moment would one advocate that playing it rough is the way to win matches. Apart from the ethics of the thing, the Wallabies have proved more than once that putting in the dirt is no formula in itself for success. But if continued winning is the object there is no question that the meek shall inherit the earth does not apply to the rugby field. A certain measure of ruthlessness, added as the extra ingredient to expertise, is essential.

It is a matter of attitude of mind. The Springboks and the All Blacks had it in their heyday. The Lions now have it. The ability to let their opponents know in no uncertain terms: 'We're dominating this match and we don't want any bloody nonsense from you, understand?'

England having done what none of the other Home Countries had ever achieved – beating New Zealand and South Africa on their home grounds – it might have been expected that they would have imposed some sort of dominance on the International championship. But their Wooden Spoon of 1974 was to be followed by another season just as humiliating.

At the start of the 1975 International campaign hopes had been high, based mainly on the fact that John Burgess, of Lancashire success, had taken over as coach and 'dynamic' was the word commonly used in describing his approach to the job. Sure enough, as preparation got under way, news came from the training camp that he was really driving the England squad towards bigger and better things.

That highly regarded pack was still basically intact, and could still be regarded – on paper – as the best in the Championship. They could get England off to a good start in the tournament by disposing of Ireland's 'Dad's Army' as Willie John McBride's pack had come to be known. But they didn't.

Then France beat England. Then Wales trounced them. And so the Twickenham fans approached the conclusion of the 1975 International proceedings – the Calcutta Cup – knowing their side had already secured the Wooden Spoon for the second year in succession and wondering whether, like the previous year, not a single match would be won.

The Rugby Union turned on two novelties for this particular England-Scotland game. One was pre-match entertainment provided by the 300-strong Marching Mizzou, an American band augmented by 'Drum Majors, Twirlers, Golden Girls and Pom Pom Girls'. The other was a jump in price for best seats to a swinging £3.50. Neither of these was viewed with any great enthusiasm by the rugby fans. They were even less enthusiastic about the match itself.

The Times headed its write-up of the game 'England Play a Tune With the Wooden Spoon', a far better headline than the match warranted. In fact England scraped home by a single point in a lack-lustre display which had their followers almost as depressed as they would have been if they had lost.

English rugby had indeed reached a new low point.

John Burgess, on such a short showing, would unfairly have been made the scapegoat. He had suffered from what that great coach Fred Allen had once promulgated: 'no amount of coaching is to any effect if you haven't the players with the talent or the will to benefit from it.'

It seemed clear that, more than anything, what England needed was new blood. And in choosing the side to tour Australia at the conclusion of the 1974–75 season, the selectors showed themselves fully alive to this fact. Twelve uncapped players were included. And surely the selectors would not again commit the crime of blooding new players only to discard them before they had had any real chance to develop in big-time rugby.

England supporters hoped that they would contribute to a resurgence and, as the second half of the 1970s progressed, that some if not all of these new names would become happily familiar to them on the International scene: Wordsworth, Hignell, Maxwell, Ashton, Kingston, Callum, Beaumont, Raphael, Blakeway, Butler, Wilkinson and Wyatt.

Facts & Figures

Five Nations Champions

Year	Champion(s)	Year	Champion(s)
1884	England	1914	England
1885*	——	1920	England, Scotland, Wales
1886	England, Scotland	1921	England
1887	Scotland	1922	Wales
1888*	——	1923	England
1889*	——	1924	England
1890	England, Scotland	1925	Scotland
1891	Scotland	1926	Scotland, Ireland
1892	England	1927	Scotland, Ireland
1893	Wales	1928	England
1894	Ireland	1929	Scotland
1895	Scotland	1930	England
1896	Ireland	1931	Wales
1897*	——	1932	England, Wales, Ireland
1898	Scotland	1933	Scotland
1899	Ireland	1934	England
1900	Wales	1935	Ireland
1901	Scotland	1936	Wales
1902	Wales	1937	England
1903	Scotland	1938	Scotland
1904	Scotland	1939	England, Wales, Ireland
1905	Wales	1947	Wales, England
1906	Ireland, Wales	1948	Ireland
1907	Scotland	1949	Ireland
1908	Wales	1950	Wales
1909	Wales		
1910	England		
1911	Wales		
1912	England, Ireland		
1913	England		

Year	Winner	Year	Winner
1951	Ireland	1962	France
1952	Wales	1963	England
1953	England	1964	Scotland, Wales
1954	England, France, Wales	1965	Wales
1955	France, Wales	1966	Wales
1956	Wales	1967	France
1957	England	1968	France
1958	England	1969	Wales
1959	France	1970	France, Wales
1960	France, England	1971	Wales
1961	France	1972*	——
		1973	Quintuple tie
		1974	Ireland
		1975	Wales

**Matches not completed, for various reasons*

Triple Crown

WINNERS TO DATE

England: 13 times – 1884, 1892, 1913, 1914, 1921, 1923, 1924, 1928, 1934, 1937, 1954, 1957, 1960.
Wales: 12 times – 1893, 1900, 1902, 1905, 1908, 1909, 1911, 1950, 1952, 1965, 1969, 1971.
Scotland: 8 times – 1891, 1895, 1901, 1903, 1907, 1925, 1933, 1938.
Ireland: 4 times – 1894, 1899, 1948, 1949.

Grand Slam

WINNERS TO DATE

England: 7 times – 1913, 1914, 1921, 1923, 1924, 1928, 1957.
Wales: 6 times – 1908, 1909, 1911, 1950, 1952, 1971.
Scotland: once – 1925.
Ireland: once – 1948.
France: once – 1968.

English International Results

Points-scoring was first introduced in 1886, when an International Board was formed by Scotland, Ireland, and Wales. Points-values varied between countries until 1890, when England agreed to join the Board, and uniform values were adopted. The table below shows points-values from the 1890–91 season onwards.

Northern hemisphere seasons	*Try*	*Conversion*	*Penalty goal*	*Dropped goal*	*Goal from mark*
1890–91	1	2	2	3	3
1891–92 to 1892–93	2	3	3	4	4
1893–94 to 1904–05	3	2	3	4	4
1905–06 to 1947–48	3	2	3	4	3
1948–49 to 1970–71	3	2	3	3	3
1971–72 to	4	2	3	3	3

ENGLAND v. SCOTLAND

Played 90 England won 42, Scotland won 34, Drawn 14

1871 Raeburn Place (Edinburgh)	*Scotland* 1G 1T to 1T
1872 The Oval (London)	*England* 2G 2T to 1G
1873 Glasgow	*Drawn* no score
1874 The Oval	*England* 1G to 1T
1875 Raeburn Place	*Drawn* no score
1876 The Oval	*England* 1G 1T to 0
1877 Raeburn Place	*Scotland* 1G to 0
1878 The Oval	*Drawn* no score
1879 Raeburn Place	*Drawn* 1G each
1880 Manchester	*England* 2G 3T to 1G
1881 Raeburn Place	*Drawn* 1G 1T each
1882 Manchester	*Scotland* 2T to 0
1883 Raeburn Place	*England* 2T to 1T
1884 Blackheath (London)	*England* 1G to 1T
1885 No Match	
1886 Raeburn Place	*Drawn* no score
1887 Manchester	*Drawn* 1T each
1888 No Match	
1889 No Match	
1890 Raeburn Place	*England* 1G 1T to 0
1891 Richmond (London)	*Scotland* 3G (9) to 1G (3)
1892 Raeburn Place	*England* 1G (5) to 0

1893	Leeds	*Scotland* 2DG (8) to 0
1894	Raeburn Place	*Scotland* 2T (6) to 0
1895	Richmond	*Scotland* 1PG 1T (6) to 1PG (3)
1896	Glasgow	*Scotland* 1G 2T (11) to 0
1897	Manchester	*England* 1G 1DG 1T (12) to 1T (3)
1898	Powderhall (Edinburgh)	*Drawn* 1T (3) each
1899	Blackheath	*Scotland* 1G (5) to 0
1900	Inverleith (Edinburgh	*Drawn* no score
1901	Blackheath	*Scotland* 3G 1T (18) to 1T (3)
1902	Inverleith	*England* 2T (6) to 1T (3)
1903	Richmond	*Scotland* 1DG 2T (10) to 2T (6)
1904	Inverleith	*Scotland* 2T (6) to 1T (3)
1905	Richmond	*Scotland* 1G 1T (8) to 0
1906	Inverleith	*England* 3T (9) to 1T (3)
1907	Blackheath	*Scotland* 2T (6) to 1T (3)
1908	Inverleith	*Scotland* 1G 2DG 1T (16) to 2G (10)
1909	Richmond	*Scotland* 3G 1T (18) to 1G 1T (8)
1910	Inverleith	*England* 1G 3T (14) to 1G (5)
1911	Twickenham	*England* 2G 1T (13) to 1G 1T (8)
1912	Inverleith	*Scotland* 1G 1T (8) to 1G (5)
1913	Twickenham	*England* 1T (3) to 0
1914	Inverleith	*England* 2G 2T (16) to 1G 1DG 2T(15)
1920	Twickenham	*England* 2G 1T (13) to 1DG (4)
1921	Inverleith	*England* 3G 1T (18) to 0
1922	Twickenham	*England* 1G 2T (11) to 1G (5)
1923	Inverleith	*England* 1G 1T (8) to 2T (6)
1924	Twickenham	*England* 3G 1DG (19) to 0
1925	Murrayfield	*Scotland* 2G 1DG (14) to 1G 1PG 1T (11)
1926	Twickenham	*Scotland* 2G 1DG 1T (17) to 3T (9)
1927	Murrayfield	*Scotland* 1G 1DG 4T (21) to 2G 1PG (13)
1928	Twickenham	*England* 2T (6) to 0
1929	Murrayfield	*Scotland* 4T (12) to 2T (6)
1930	Twickenham	*Drawn* no score
1931	Murrayfield	*Scotland* 5G 1T (28) to 2G 1PG 2T (19)
1932	Twickenham	*England* 2G 2T (16) to 1T (3)
1933	Murrayfield	*Scotland* 1T (3) to 0
1934	Twickenham	*England* 2T (6) to 1T (3)
1935	Murrayfield	*Scotland* 2G (10) to 1DG 1T (7)
1936	Twickenham	*England* 3T (9) to 1G 1PG (8)
1937	Murrayfield	*England* 2T (6) to 1PG (3)
1938	Twickenham	*Scotland* 2PG 5T (21) to 1DG 3PG 1T (16)
1939	Murrayfield	*England* 3PG (9) to 2T (6)
1947	Twickenham	*England* 4G 1DG (24) to 1G (5)
1948	Murrayfield	*Scotland* 2T (6) to 1PG (3)
1949	Twickenham	*England* 2G 3T (19) to 1PG (3)
1950	Murrayfield	*Scotland* 2G 1T (13) to 1G 1PG 1T (11)
1951	Twickenham	*England* 1G (5) to 1T (3)
1952	Murrayfield	*England* 2G 1DG 2T (19) to 1T (3)

1953 Twickenham	*England* 4G 2T (26) to 1G 1T (8)
1954 Murrayfield	*England* 2G 1T (13) to 1T (3)
1955 Twickenham	*England* 1PG 2T (9) to 1PG 1T (6)
1956 Murrayfield	*England* 1G 2PG (11) to 1PG 1T (6)
1957 Twickenham	*England* 2G 1PG 1T (16) to 1PG (3)
1958 Murrayfield	*Drawn* 1PG (3) each
1959 Twickenham	*Drawn* 1PG (3) each
1960 Murrayfield	*England* 3G 1DG 1PG (21)to 3PG 1T (12)
1961 Twickenham	*England* 1PG 1T (6) to 0
1962 Murrayfield	*Drawn* 1PG (3) each
1963 Twickenham	*England* 2G (10) to 1G 1DG (8)
1964 Murrayfield	*Scotland* 3G (15) to 1PG 1T (6)
1965 Twickenham	*Drawn* England 1T (3) Scotland 1DG (3)
1966 Murrayfield	*Scotland* 1PG 1T (6) to 1DG (3)
1967 Twickenham	*England* 3G 2PG 1DG 1T (27) to 1G 2PG 1T (14)
1968 Murrayfield	*England* 1G 1PG (8) to 1PG 1D (6)
1969 Twickenham	*England* 1G 1T (8) to 1PG (3)
1970 Murrayfield	*Scotland* 1G 2PG 1T (14) to 1G (5)
1971 Twickenham	*Scotland* 2G 1DG 1T (16) to 3PG 2T (15)
*1971 Murrayfield	*Scotland* 4G 1PG 1T (26) to 1PG 1DG (6)
1972 Murrayfield	*Scotland* 4PG 1DG 2T (23) to 3PG (9)
1973 Twickenham	*England* 2G 2T (20) to 1G 1PG 1T (13)
1974 Murrayfield	*Scotland* 1G 2PG 1T (16) to 1DG 1PG 2T (14)
1975 Twickenham	*England* 1PG 1T (7) to 2PG (6)

**Special Centenary match – non-championship*

ENGLAND v. IRELAND

Played 86 England won 49, Ireland won 29, Drawn 8

1875 The Oval (London)	*England* 2G 1T to 0
1876 Dublin	*England* 1G 1T to 0
1877 The Oval	*England* 2G 2T to 0
1878 Dublin	*England* 2G 1T to 0
1879 The Oval	*England* 3G 2T to 0
1880 Dublin	*England* 1G 1T to 1T
1881 Manchester	*England* 2G 2T to 0
1882 Dublin	*Drawn* 2T each
1883 Manchester	*England* 1G 3T to 1T
1884 Dublin	*England* 1G to 0
1885 Manchester	*England* 2T to 1T
1886 Dublin	*England* 1T to 0
1887 Dublin	*Ireland* 2G to 0
1888 No Match	
1889 No Match	
1890 Blackheath (London)	*England* 3T to 0
1891 Dublin	*England* 2G 3T (9) to 0
1892 Manchester	*England* 1G 1T (7) to 0

1893 Dublin	*England* 2T (4) to 0
1894 Blackheath	*Ireland* 1DG 1T (7) to 1G (5)
1895 Dublin	*England* 2T (6) to 1T (3)
1896 Leeds	*Ireland* 2G (10) to 1DG (4)
1897 Dublin	*Ireland* 1DG 3T (13) to 2PG 1T (9)
1898 Richmond (London)	*Ireland* 1PG 2T (9) to 1PG 1T (6)
1899 Dublin	*Ireland* 1PG 1T (6) to 0
1900 Richmond	*England* 1G 1DG 2T (15) to 1DG (4)
1901 Dublin	*Ireland* 2G (10) to 1PG 1T (6)
1902 Leicester	*England* 2T (6) to 1T (3)
1903 Dublin	*Ireland* 1PG 1T (6) to 0
1904 Blackheath	*England* 2G 3T (19) to 0
1905 Cork	*Ireland* 1G 4T (17) to 1T (3)
1906 Leicester	*Ireland* 2G 2T (16) to 2T (6)
1907 Dublin	*Ireland* 1G 1GM 3T (17) to 1PG 2T (9)
1908 Richmond	*England* 2G 1T (13) to 1PG (3)
1909 Dublin	*England* 1G 2T (11) to 1G (5)
1910 Twickenham	*Drawn* no score
1911 Dublin	*Ireland* 1T (3) to 0
1912 Twickenham	*England* 5T (15) to 0
1913 Dublin	*England* 1PG 4T (15) to 1DG (4)
1914 Twickenham	*England* 1G 4T (17) to 1G 1DG 1T (12)
1920 Dublin	*England* 1G 3T (14) to 1G 1PG 1T (11)
1921 Twickenham	*England* 1G 1DG 2T (15) to 0
1922 Dublin	*England* 4T (12) to 1T (3)
1923 Leicester	*England* 2G 1DG 3T (23) to 1G (5)
1924 Belfast	*England* 1G 3T (14) to 1T (3)
1925 Twickenham	*Drawn* 2T (6) each
1926 Dublin	*Ireland* 2G 1PG 2T (19) to 3G (15)
1927 Twickenham	*England* 1G 1T (8) to 1PG 1T (6)
1928 Dublin	*England* 1DG 1T (7) to 2T (6)
1929 Twickenham	*Ireland* 2T (6) to 1G (5)
1930 Dublin	*Ireland* 1DG (4) to 1T (3)
1931 Twickenham	*Ireland* 1PG 1T (6) to 1G (5)
1932 Dublin	*England* 1G 2PG (11) to 1G 1PG (8)
1933 Twickenham	*England* 1G 4T (17) to 1PG 1T (6)
1934 Dublin	*England* 2G 1T (13) to 1T (3)
1935 Twickenham	*England* 1G 3PG (14) to 1T (3)
1936 Dublin	*Ireland* 2T (6) to 1T (3)
1937 Twickenham	*England* 1PG 2T (9) to 1G 1T (8)
1938 Dublin	*England* 6G 1PG 1T (36) to 1G 3T (14)
1939 Twickenham	*Ireland* 1G (5) to 0
1947 Dublin	*Ireland* 2G 1PG 3T (22) to 0
1948 Twickenham	*Ireland* 1G 2T (11) to 2G (10)
1949 Dublin	*Ireland* 1G 2PG 1T (14) to 1G (5)
1950 Twickenham	*England* 1T (3) to 0
1951 Dublin	*Ireland* 1PG (3) to 0
1952 Twickenham	*England* 1T (3) to 0

1953 Dublin	*Drawn* 2PG 1T (9) each
1954 Twickenham	*England* 1G 1PG 2T (14) to 1PG (3)
1955 Dublin	*Drawn* Ireland 1PG 1T (6) England 2T (6)
1956 Twickenham	*England* 1G 3PG 2T (20) to 0
1957 Dublin	*England* 1PG 1T (6) to 0
1958 Twickenham	*England* 1PG 1T (6) to 0
1959 Dublin	*England* 1PG (3) to 0
1960 Twickenham	*England* 1G 1DG (8) to 1G (5)
1961 Dublin	*Ireland* 1G 2PG (11) to 1G 1T (8)
1962 Twickenham	*England* 2G 1PG 1T (16) to 0
1963 Dublin	*Drawn* no score
1964 Twickenham	*Ireland* 3G 1T (18) to 1G (5)
1965 Dublin	*Ireland* 1G (5) to 0
1966 Twickenham	*Drawn* 1PG 1T (6) each
1967 Dublin	*England* 1G 1PG (8) to 1PG (3)
1968 Twickenham	*Drawn* England 2PG 1DG (9) Ireland 3PG (9)
1969 Dublin	*Ireland* 1G 2PG 1DG 1T (17) to 4PG 1T (15)
1970 Twickenham	*England* 2DG 1T (9) to 1PG (3)
1971 Dublin	*England* 3PG (9) to 2T (6)
1972 Twickenham	*Ireland* 1G 1DG 1PG 1T (16) to 1G 2PH (12)
1973 Dublin	*Ireland* 2G 1PG 1DG (18) to 1G 1PG (9)
1974 Twickenham	*Ireland* 2G 1PG 1DG 2T (26) to 1G 5PG (21)
1975 Dublin	*Ireland* 2G (12) to 1G 1PG (9)

ENGLAND v. WALES

Played 79 England won 33, Wales won 35, Drawn 11

1881 Blackheath (London)	*England* 7 1DG 5T to 0
1882 No Match	
1883 Swansea	*England* 2G 4T to 0
1884 Leeds	*England* 1G 2T to 1G
1885 Swansea	*England* 1G 4T to 1G 1T
1886 Blackheath	*England* 1G 2T to 1G
1887 Llanelli	*Drawn* no score
1888 No Match	
1889 No Match	
1890 Dewsbury	*Wales* 1T to 0
1891 Newport	*England* 2G 1T (7) to 1G (3)
1892 Blackheath	*England* 3G 1T (17) to 0
1893 Cardiff	*Wales* 1G 1PG 2T (14) to 1G 3T (11)
1894 Birkenhead	*England* 4G 1GM (24) to 1T (3)
1895 Swansea	*England* 1G 3T (14) to 2T (6)
1896 Blackheath	*England* 2G 5T (25) to 0
1897 Newport	*Wales* 1G 2T (11) to 0
1898 Blackheath	*England* 1G 3T (14) to 1DG 1T (7)
1899 Swansea	*Wales* 4G 2T (26) to 1T (3)
1900 Gloucester	*Wales* 2G 1PG (13) to 1T (3)
1901 Cardiff	*Wales* 2G 1T (13) to 0

1902 Blackheath	*Wales* 1PG 2T (9) to 1G 1T (8)
1903 Swansea	*Wales* 3G 2T (21) to 1G (5)
1904 Leicester	*Drawn* England 1G 1PG 2T (14) Wales 2G 1GM (14)
1905 Cardiff	*Wales* 2G 5T (25) to 0
1906 Richmond (London)	*Wales* 2G 2T (16) to 1T (3)
1907 Swansea	*Wales* 2G 4T (22) to 0
1908 Bristol	*Wales* 3G 1DG 1PG 2T (28) to 3G 1T (18)
1909 Cardiff	*Wales* 1G 1T (8) to 0
1910 Twickenham	*England* 1G 1PG 1T (11) to 2T (6)
1911 Swansea	*Wales* 1PG 4T (15) to 1G 2T (11)
1912 Twickenham	*England* 1G 1T (8) to 0
1913 Cardiff	*England* 1G 1DG 1T (12) to 0
1914 Twickenham	*England* 2G (10) to 1G 1DG (9)
1920 Swansea	*Wales* 1G 2DG 1PG 1T (19) to 1G (5)
1921 Twickenham	*England* 1G 1DG 3T (18) to 1T (3)
1922 Cardiff	*Wales* 2G 6T (28) to 2T (6)
1923 Twickenham	*England* 1DG 1T (7) to 1T (3)
1924 Swansea	*England* 1G 4T (17) to 3T (9)
1925 Twickenham	*England* 1PG 3T (12) to 2T (6)
1926 Cardiff	*Drawn* 1T (3) each
1927 Twickenham	*England* 1G 1PG 1GM (11) to 1PG 2T (9)
1928 Swansea	*England* 2G (10) to 1G 1T (8)
1929 Twickenham	*England* 1G 1T (8) to 1T (3)
1930 Cardiff	*England* 1G 1PG 1T (11) to 1T (3)
1931 Twickenham	*Drawn* England 1G 2PG (11) Wales 1G 1GM 1T (11)
1932 Swansea	*Wales* 1G 1DG 1PG (12) to 1G (5)
1933 Twickenham	*Wales* 1DG 1T (7) to 1T (3)
1934 Cardiff	*England* 3T (9) to 0
1935 Twickenham	*Drawn* England 1PG (3) Wales 1T (3)
1936 Swansea	*Drawn* no score
1937 Twickenham	*England* 1DG (4) to 1T (3)
1938 Cardiff	*Wales* 1G 2PG 1T (14) to 1G 1T (8)
1939 Twickenham	*England* 1T (3) to 0
1947 Cardiff	*England* 1G 1DG (9) to 2T (6)
1948 Twickenham	*Drawn* England 1PG (3) Wales 1T (3)
1949 Cardiff	*Wales* 3T (9) to 1DG (3)
1950 Twickenham	*Wales* 1G 1PG 1T (11) to 1G (5)
1951 Swansea	*Wales* 4G 1T (23) to 1G (5)
1952 Twickenham	*Wales* 1G 1T (8) to 2T (6)
1953 Cardiff	*England* 1G 1PG (8) to 1PG (3)
1954 Twickenham	*England* 3T (9) to 1PG 1T (6)
1955 Cardiff	*Wales* 1PG (3) to 0
1956 Twickenham	*Wales* 1G 1T (8) to 1PG (3)
1957 Cardiff	*England* 1PG (3) to 0
1958 Twickenham	*Drawn* England 1T (3) Wales 1PG (3)
1959 Cardiff	*Wales* 1G (5) to 0
1960 Twickenham	*England* 1G 2PG 1T (14) to 2PG (6)
1961 Cardiff	*Wales* 2T (6) to 1T (3)

1962 Twickenham	*Drawn* no score
1963 Cardiff	*England* 2G 1DG (13) to 1PG 1T (6)
1964 Twickenham	*Drawn* 2T (6) each
1965 Cardiff	*Wales* 1G 1DG 2T (14) to 1PG (3)
1966 Twickenham	*Wales* 1G 2PG (11) to 1PG 1T (6)
1967 Cardiff	*Wales* 5G 2PG 1DG (34) to 4PG 3T (21)
1968 Twickenham	*wn* England 1G 1PG 1T (11) Wales 1G 1DG 1T (11)
1969 Cardiff	*Wales* 3G 2PG 1DG 2T (30) to 3PG (9)
1970 Twickenham	*Wales* 1G 1DG 3T (17) to 2G 1PG (13)
1971 Cardiff	*Wales* 2G 2DG 1P 1T (22) to 1P 1T (6)
1972 Twickenham	*Wales* 1G 2PG (12) to 1PG (3)
1973 Cardiff	*Wales* 1G 1PG 4T (25) to 2PG 1DG (9)
1974 Twickenham	*England* 1G 2PG 1T (16) to 1G 2PG (12)
1975 Cardiff	*Wales* 1G 2PG 2T (20) to 1T (4)

ENGLAND v. FRANCE

Played 49 England won 29, France won 14, Drawn 6

1906 Paris	*England* 4G 5T (35) to 1G 1T (8)
1907 Richmond (London)	*England* 5G 1DG 4T (41) to 2G 1PG (13)
1908 Paris	*England* 2G 3T (19) to 0
1909 Leicester	*England* 2G 4T (22) to 0
1910 Paris	*England* 1G 2T (11) to 1T (3)
1911 Twickenham	*England* 5G 2PG 2T (37) to 0
1912 Paris	*England* 1G 1DG 3T (18) to 1G 1T (8)
1913 Twickenham	*England* 1G 5T (20) to 0
1914 Paris	*England* 6G 3T (39) to 2G 1T (13)
1920 Twickenham	*England* 1G 1PG (8) to 1T (3)
1921 Paris	*England* 2G (10) to 2PG (6)
1922 Twickenham	*Drawn* England 1G 2PG (11) France 1G 2T (11)
1923 Paris	*England* 1G 1DG 1T (12) to 1PG (3)
1924 Twickenham	*England* 2G 3T (19) to 1DG 1T (7)
1925 Paris	*England* 2G 1GM (13) to 1G 2T (11)
1926 Twickenham	*England* 1G 2T (11) to 0
1927 Paris	*France* 1T (3) to 0
1928 Twickenham	*England* 3G 1T (18) to 1G 1T (8)
1929 Paris	*England* 2G 2T (16) to 2T (6)
1930 Twickenham	*England* 1G 2T (11) to 1G (5)
1931 Paris	*France* 2DG 2T (14) to 2G 1T (13)
1947 Twickenham	*England* 2T (6) to 1PG (3)
1948 Paris	*France* 1G 1DG 2T (15) to 0
1949 Twickenham	*England* 1G 1DG (8) to 1DG (3)
1950 Paris	*France* 2T (6) to 1T (3)
1951 Twickenham	*France* 1G 1PG 1T (11) to 1T (3)
1952 Paris	*England* 2PG (6) to 1T (3)
1953 Twickenham	*England* 1G 2T (11) to 0
1954 Paris	*France* 1G 1DG 1T (11) to 1T (3)

1955 Twickenham *France* 2G 2DG (16) to 2PG 1T (9)
1956 Paris *France* 1G 2PG 1T (14) to 2PG 1T (9)
1957 Twickenham *England* 3T (9) to 1G (5)
1958 Paris *England* 1G 1PG 2T (14) to 0
1959 Twickenham *Drawn* 1PG (3) each
1960 Paris *Drawn* France 1PG (3) England 1T (3)
1961 Twickenham *Drawn* 1G (5) each
1962 Paris *France* 2G 1T (13) to 0
1963 Twickenham *England* 2PG (6) to 1G (5)
1964 Paris *England* 1PG 1T (6) to 1T (3)
1965 Twickenham *England* 2PG 1T (9) to 1PG 1T (6)
1966 Paris *France* 2G 1T (13) to 0
1967 Twickenham *France* 2G 1DG 1PG (16) to 3PG 1DG (12)
1968 Paris *France* 1G 2DG 1PG (14) to 1DG 2PG (9)
1969 Twickenham *England* 2G 3PG 1T (22) to 1DG (8)
1970 Paris *France* 4G 2DG 1PG 2T (35) to 2G 1PG (13)
1971 Twickenham
Drawn England 1G 3PG (14) France 1G 1PG 1DG 1T (14)
1972 Paris *France* 5G 1PG 1T (37) to 1G 2PG (12)
1973 Twickenham *England* 2PG 2T (14) to 1G (6)
1974 Paris *Drawn* 1G 1PG 1DG (12) each
1975 Twickenham *France* 4G 1PG (27) to 4PG 2T (20)

ENGLAND v. NEW ZEALAND

Played 10 England won 2, New Zealand won 8, Drawn 0

1905 Crystal Palace (London) *New Zealand* 5T (15) to 0
1925 Twickenham *New Zealand* 1G 1PG 3T (17) to 1G 1PG 1T (11)
1936 Twickenham *England* 1DG 3T (13) to 0
1954 Twickenham *New Zealand* 1G (5) to 0
1963 *1* Auckland *New Zealand* 3G 1DG 1PG (21) to 1G 2PG (11)
2 Christchurch *New Zealand* 1GM 2T (9) to 1P G1T (6)
New Zealand won series 2–0
1964 Twickenham *New Zealand* 1G 2PG 1T (14) to 0
1967 Twickenham *New Zealand* 4G 1T (23) to 1G 1PG 1T (11)
1973 Twickenham *New Zealand* 1G 1DG (9) to 0
1973 Auckland *England* 2G 1T (16) to 1G 1T (10)

ENGLAND v. SOUTH AFRICA

Played 7 England won 2, South Africa won 4, Drawn 1

1906 Crystal Palace (London) *Drawn* 1T (3) each
1913 Twickenham *South Africa* 2PG 1T (9) to 1T (3)
1932 Twickenham *South Africa* 1DG 1T (7) to 0
1952 Twickenham *South Africa* 1G 1PG (8) to 1T (3)
1961 Twickenham *South Africa* 1G (5) to 0
1969 Twickenham *England* 1G 1PG 1T (11) to 1G 1PG (8)
1972 Johannesburg *England* 1G 4PG (18) to 3PG (9)

ENGLAND v. AUSTRALIA

Played 6 England won 2, Australia won 4, Drawn 0

1909 Blackheath (London)	*Australia* 3T (9) to 1T (3)
1948 Twickenham	*Australia* 1G 2T (11) to 0
1958 Twickenham	*England* 1PG 2T (9) to 1DG 1PG (6)
1963 Sydney	*Australia* 3G 1T (18) to 3T (9)
1967 Twickenham	*Australia* 1G 3DG 2PG 1T (23) to 1G 2PG (11)
1973 Twickenham	*England* 1G 2PG 2T (20) to 1PG (3)

England Against the Major Overseas Countries

v. NEW ZEALAND

	Played	*Won*	*Lost*	*Drawn*	*Points For*	*Points Against*
At Home	7	1	6	–	35	83
On Tour	3	1	2	–	33	40

v. AUSTRALIA

	Played	*Won*	*Lost*	*Drawn*	*Points For*	*Points Against*
At Home	5	2	3	–	43	52
On Tour	1	–	1	–	9	18

v. SOUTH AFRICA

	Played	*Won*	*Lost*	*Drawn*	*Points For*	*Points Against*
At Home	6	1	4	–	20	40
On Tour	1	1	–	–	18	9

TOTALS

	Played	*Won*	*Lost*	*Drawn*	*Points For*	*Points Against*
At Home	18	4	13	1	98	175
On Tour	5	2	3	–	60	67
	23	6	16	1	158	242

England Against the Visitors

(Chapter 9)

Year	*Opponents*	*Won*	*Lost*
1889	N.Z. Native Team	England 17–0	
1905	New Zealand		0–15 New Zealand
1906	South Africa		3–3 *Drawn*
1909	Australia		3–9 Australia
1913	South Africa		3–9 South Africa
1925	New Zealand		11–17 New Zealand
1928	New South Wales	England 18–8	
1932	South Africa		0–7 South Africa
1936	New Zealand	England 13–0	
1948	Australia		0–11 Australia
1952	South Africa		3–8 South Africa
1954	New Zealand		0–5 New Zealand
1958	Australia	England 9–6	
1961	South Africa		0–5 South Africa
1964	New Zealand		0–14 New Zealand
1967	Australia		11–23 Australia
1967	New Zealand		11–23 New Zealand
1969	South Africa	England 11–8	
1971	Overseas XV		11–28 Overseas XV
1973	New Zealand		0–9 New Zealand
1973	Australia	England 20–3	

Played 21, Won 5, Lost 14, Drawn 1 Points: For 141, Against 218

England on Tour

(Chapter 11)

Year	*Opponents*	*Won*	*Lost*
1963	New Zealand		11–21 New Zealand
	New Zealand		6–9 New Zealand
	Australia		9–18 Australia
1972	South Africa	England 18–9	
1973	New Zealand	England 16–10	

Played 5, Won 2, Lost 3 Points: For 60, Against 67

ENGLAND TEAM RECORDS

Highest score

41 v. France (41–13) 1907 Richmond

v. individual countries

27 v. Scotland (27–14) 1967 Twickenham

36 v. Ireland (36–14) 1938 Dublin

25 v. Wales (25–0) 1896 Blackheath (London)

41 v. France (41–13) 1907 Richmond

16 v. N. Zealand (16–10) 1973 Auckland

18 v. S. Africa (18–9) 1972 Johannesburg

20 v. Australia (20–3) 1973 Twickenham

Biggest winning points margin

37 v. France (37–0) 1911 Twickenham

v. individual countries

19 v. Scotland (19–0) 1924 Twickenham

22 v. Ireland (36–14) 1938 Dublin

25 v. Wales (25–0) 1896 Blackheath

37 v. France (37–0) 1911 Twickenham

13 v. N. Zewland (13–0) 1936 Twickenham

9 v. S. Africa (18–9) 1972 Johannesburg

17 v. Australia (20–3) 1973 Twickenham

Highest score by opposing team

37 France (12–37) 1972 Colombes (Paris)

by individual countries

28 Scotland (19–28) 1938 Murrayfield

26 Ireland (21–26) 1974 Twickenham

34 Wales (21–34) 1967 Cardiff

37 France (12–37) 1972 Colombes

23 N. Zealand (11–23) 1967 Twickenham

9 S. Africa { (3–9) 1913 Twickenham; (18–9) 1972 Johannesburg }

23 Australia (11–23) 1967 Twickenham

Biggest losing points margin

25 { v. Wales (0–25) 1905 Cardiff; v. France (12–37) 1972 Colombes }

v. individual countries

20 v. Scotland (6–26) 1971 Murrayfield

22 v. Ireland (0–22) 1947 Dublin

25 v. Wales (0–25) 1905 Cardiff

25 v. France (12–37) 1972 Colombes

15 v. N. Zealand (0–15) 1906 Crystal Palace (London)

7 v. S. Africa (0–7) 1932 Twickenham

12 v. Australia (11–23) 1967 Twickenham

Most tries by England in a match

9 { v. France (35–8) 1906 Parc des Princes (Paris); v. France (41–13) 1907 Richmond; v. France (39–13) 1914 Colombes }

Most tries againt England in a match

8 by Wales (6–28) 1922 Cardiff

INDIVIDUAL RECORDS

Most capped player
J. V. Pullin 39 1966–74
in individual positions
Full-back
R. B. Hiller 19 1968–72
Wing
C. N. Lowe 25 1913–23
Centre
J. Butterfield 28 1953–59
Fly-half
W. J. A. Davies 22 1913–23
Scrum-half
R. E. G. Jeeps 24 1956–62
Prop
C. R. Jacobs 29 1956–64
Hooker
J. V. Pullin 39 1966–74
Lock
J. D. Currie 25 1956–62
Flanker
D P. Rogers 34 1961–69
No. 8
J. McG. K. Kendall-Carpenter
18 (23) 1949–54

David Duckham, England's most capped back, has played 14 times at centre, and 19 times on the wing, a total of 33 caps. M. P. Weston won 5 of his 29 caps at fly-half
W. W. Wakefield won his 31 caps variously at prop, lock, and No. 8
R. Cove-Smith, 29 caps, played 22 times at lock and 7 times at No. 8
Kendall-Carpenter played 5 times as prop
G. S. Conway won most of his 18 caps at No. 8, but also played at prop

Most points for England – 138
R. B. Hiller (19 appearances) 1968–72

Most points in a match – 22
D. Lambert v. France 1911 Twickenham

Most tries for England – 13
J. G. G. Birkett 1906–12

Most tries in a match – 4
A. Hudson v. France 1906 Parc des Princes
D. Lambert v. France 1907 Richmond

Most points in International Championship in a season – 38
R. W. Hosen 1966–67

Most points in any tour match – 24
A. G. B. Old v. Griqualand West 1972 Kimberley

NOTE: Statistics apply up to conclusion of 1974 International season.

Index